THE TRUTH ABOUT THE
WEST AFRICAN LAND QUESTION

THE TRUTH ABOUT THE
WEST AFRICAN LAND QUESTION

BY
CASELY HAYFORD
(EKRA-AGIMAN)
*of the Inner Temple, Esquire, Barrister-at-law, and of the
Gold Coast Bar.*

NEGRO UNIVERSITIES PRESS
NEW YORK

45- 47842

Originally published in 1913
by C. M. Phillips, London

Reprinted 1969 by
Negro Universities Press
A DIVISION OF GREENWOOD PUBLISHING CORP.
NEW YORK

SBN 8371-1393-8

PRINTED IN UNITED STATES OF AMERICA

TO

UNITED WEST AFRICA

THIS WORK

IS

HOPEFULLY INSCRIBED.

CONTENTS.

" *In West Africa, the circumstances being what they are, interference with native property is bound to affect, not in theory but in practice, the interest of every single individual in the country. In respect to the native law of land tenure, we are not confronted with any evil. On the contrary, the system of native land tenure is essentially just, thoroughly adapted to the need of the country and its people, a striking refutation of the arrested development theory' as applied to the Negro, and per se an eloquent vindication of the Negro's claim to consideration at the hands of the European invaders of, and settlers in, his country. There can be no justification whatever for the break-up of land tenure, or for the alienation of native property, under any pretext. It is morally indefensible, and what is morally indefensible is seldom politically wise.*"—E. D. MOREL.*

* * * *

" *The Concessions Ordinance must rank as the most equitable legislative measure for the protection and preservation of native land tenure which exists in West Africa.*"—E. D. MOREL.

* * * *

" *If the native can feel that he is secure in his tenure of land, he will become a willing and eager co-operator. Moreover, it is not property alone which must be respected. Local customs, special religious ideas, necessitate the same respect on our part. Why not act in this way? What should we say if to-morrow, in Brittany or Gascony, a stronger Power arrogated to itself the right of forcing its personal habits and its special religious views upon us?*"

* * * *

" *However highly placed he may be I will break any official who commits abuses. I have already given precise and severe instructions to that effect: perhaps my tone has been harsh but my office is far from the colonies. I wish to be listened to and I think I have been understood.*" —Interview with the French Colonial Minister, quoted in the West African Mail, August 24, 1906.

The Truth about the West African Land Question.

CHAPTER I.

SOME OPENING CONSIDERATIONS.

THE present West African Land question has largely grown around the Gold Coast Land question. When you have broadly stated the truth about the latter, it may be taken as an index to the solution of the whole.

The opinion is current in certain quarters that West African intelligence is incapable of grasping the danger of the economic pressure which the influx of European capital into the country must produce. It is even assumed that such intelligence would willingly minimise the evil for pecuniary gain. A greater mistake could not be made. Indeed, no one can understand the nature of the problem better than West Africans themselves. It affects them vitally. It appeals to them in a manner that is not likely to do to a mere outsider. It touches them in a way that is not conventionally brought before the public. Hence has arisen the necessity to educate public opinion, lest in the eagerness to save the indigenes from the coils of European capital, a worse evil may be inflicted upon them.

Now, what is the crux of this land question? Is it, in the main, that the land shall belong to the indigenes and not to foreign capitalists; or that, in the last analysis, neither the foreign capitalist, nor the indigenes, but Government shall own it? To state the problem in another way, is it that the people shall be free to till the soil in their own right and sell the produce thereof to merchants abroad, the Supreme Court protecting the rights of contractor and contractee in common; or that Government shall step in and control private rights on the assumption that parties are incapable of managing their own business? The latter position is apparently the one taken up by " E.D.M." and his supporters; and it is unfortunate that no statement of the West African land question can be even partially complete without a direct reference to the personal views of " E.D.M." upon the matter. The assumption has a taint about it. For, with the best of intentions, even protection can be overdone. In the present case it looks, indeed, as if the wish were father to the thought. In fact, when you have examined the evidence, you cannot help coming to that conclusion.

One is tempted to think that the type of African dear to " E.D.M.'s " heart is the one which graces the cover of the *African Mail*. We hope we do not do him an injustice. To judge from his strictures on " educated natives " and " coast Barristers," indeed, we must be right. Even among this class are there not some honest men likely to be sufficiently disinterested to point the true way to the people? Facts are potent things. Mr. Morel and his supporters have had to admit that the Forest Bill was a clumsily-got-up measure. That was after the event. It was not until the " educated native " and the " coast Barristers " had pressed home the facts of the nature of British relations with the Gold Coast and

the injustice of compulsory acquisition of the
people's lands, or acquiring them by leaseholds,
for the purpose of forest reservations, that the admis-
sion came.   It came too late to sustain the infallibility of even " E.D.M."   We fear the able editor
of the *African Mail* is troubled with a consciousness
of the essential inferiority of the black man.   It
seems as though, where his own pet ideas are concerned, he cannot brook initiation, or the assertion
of individuality, on the part of the African.   Hence
this frequent cry of " the educated African."   In
September, 1905, public events on the Gold Coast
led me to write in the local press as follows :—" We
feel, secondly, that the educated native is unduly
maligned for party purposes.   It is the same cry as
the educated Welsh, Irish, or Scotch.   In any case,
it is a childish cry—a sign of weakness.   Does a
native cease to be a native when once he is educated?
.   .   .   .   But for the educated native, where would
the unsophisticated native be?   Hence the weakness
of the cry—the shibboleth of ' the educated native.'
Heaven grant that the educated native may never be
wanting in his duty to his less privileged brethren, or
betray their trust in him."   But, in any case, it is
wise to look at facts squarely in the face; and the
truth is that the type of African our philanthropic
friends are accustomed to has no existence to-day in
British West Africa.   The old type may, or may not,
have been doomed to perpetual servitude.   To keep
it to its lot, it might have the shadow of ownership.
As for the substance, the right of control, that must
be reserved for the so-called supreme Chief, the
protector, his good friend.   Is the Congo type, after
all, for ever to persist?   Will it always be represented as wearing a bit of coral round the neck, the
obedient hewer of wood and drawer of water for all
time?   Will its mental horizon ever lift?   Has it
even now lifted?   In the basin of the Niger Africans

have before now founded universities, and pursued knowledge for its own sake. The suggestion is, that on no account, in West Africa, must a landlord class be permitted. If it is seriously made, it presupposes a condition of perpetual servitude. It implies turning owners into serfs. It suggests violence and reprisal. It connotes might in the place of right.

There are two kinds of tyrannies with which West Africa is afflicted : the tyranny of the capitalist, and the tyranny of the philanthropist. There may be minor ones, but these are prime factors. And of all tyrannies the worst is that of one's household. "E.D.M." prides himself as Africa's own. At least, once he did. But yesterday he might have taken Africa in the hollow of his hand, and done with her as he would. To-day his lightest word is borne with suspicion and distrust. And why? Because West Africa has found to her hurt that it is within the power of philanthropy to kill, or make alive. One cannot help thinking of what has happened in South Africa in the name of philanthropy. White South Africa is all right. Black South Africa to-day is well-nigh an impossibility. Before the war the black man was the pet of the family. The high priests of philanthropy could not croon over him sufficiently. That was the beginning of the century. By 1906 Black South Africa was bleeding almost from every pore. At least, so shows the "Report of the Native Affairs Commission" (C.D. 3,889). One part of it shows the people apprehensive of the alienation of their lands for European occupation. This is characterised by the report as "a policy which, undoubtedly, contains the germs of unrest." Neither in Europe, nor in Africa, can you touch people's proprietary rights without creating a condition of doubt and unrest. You may preach until you are red in the face. You may prove that your intentions are honest. You may even command apparent acquiescence. But at heart you will still be mistrusted and taken for an impostor. "As nothing is to be gained by reticence," says the Report, "the opinion is here expressed that the chasm between the races has been broadening for years, and that the attitude of the natives is now one of distance and distrust." It has not come to that in West Africa. It is possible for meddlesome philanthropy to force the pace. Here, as there, nothing can be gained by reticence. In giving evidence one Governor averred that there was no policy at all. That accounts for it. Statesmanship has not yet made up its mind as to what place in the black man's country to assign the black man. It is in a state of expectancy. It hopes against hope that in the order of Providence something will happen to work in proprietary control. It is not stated in so many words. But the actual facts show it. Hence it is that Black South Africa is in a delirium of suspense. That is the reason why West Africa is threatened with the fever of unrest. The pity of it is that no one else is supposed to know the remedy except the very ones who have forced on the situation.

The Governor of Natal is described in the Report as the "Supreme Chief over the Native Population." It may be that gives an idea as to the aim of statesmanship. Colonial statesmanship originates from Downing Street. As in South Africa, so may it be in the West. To West African ears, however, the title sounds strange. A supreme white Chief is incongruous. The atmosphere in which West Africa had been trained had nothing of the white Chief in it. It was always the Great White Queen who did not need to be a Chief at all. Yet was she so big, so ideally high, so absolutely just, so great in tradi-

tion as to ensure the *Pax Britannica*. It was without
effort. It was done by the talisman of sheer
imagination and sympathy. Were Colonial Office
statesmanship sympathetically imaginative, it would
find a policy ready to hand. For the present let us
pursue the lessons of history. Africa north yields
her quota. If the place of South Africa is among
the serfs of the earth, hardly is that of native Egypt
better. True, she has her Khedive. But that does
not prevent her being swathed in the mocking
habiliments of philanthropy. It is this which is kill-
ing the soul of Egypt. There is a real Egypt,
and there is a false Egypt. The Egypt of the official
and of diplomacy is a false one. The true Egypt is
that which represents the soul of the people, with
its striving and yearning after a national integrity
which once was hers. The vicissitudes of Egypt are
in men's mouths. There are various versions extant.
They may all be true. They may all be false. But
there is no denying the fact that native Egypt groans
under burdens imposed by philanthropy. We may
pretend not to see these things. We may elect not
to know them. But we cannot prevent people thinking and drawing conclusions. And some of the facts
are decidedly ugly. A greater than any who, of late,
have prated about Africa has something to say upon
this matter. " The philanthropist is a person who
loves man; but he or she is frequently no better than
people who kill lap-dogs by over-feeding, or who
shut up skylarks in cages; while it is quite conceivable to me, for example, that a missionary could kill
a man to save his soul, a philanthropist kills his soul
to save his life, and there is in this a difference."
That was written by the late Mary Kingsley, a name
at mention of which sensible Africans are wont to
rise, as our manner is, in token of respect and gratitude. She was reflecting on the ways of managing
West Africa. We say that the methods that are

being recommended for adoption in respect of West Africa by " E.D.M." and his supporters are sure to kill her soul to save her life. There is a proper and a natural relation of the Government to the West African peoples. It is one of mutual trust and confidence. A trust that will promote reliance on the Supreme Court to adjust the relations between capital and native land-owners; a confidence that will ensure that Government shall not take advantage of artificial conditions and acquire overlordship, or ownership of the people's lands. Back to the land, say all forward movements. It suggests a condition in which the cultivator will really and truly be master of the soil. Such security is ensured by the native system. At least, so it is on the Gold Coast. Why disturb it? Why introduce measures which will assuredly shake their institutions to the very foundations, and break up their social organisations?

Mr. Morel's position in this controversy is ambiguous. He holds a brief for West Africa. At least, he makes it to appear so. Most distinctly does he hold a brief for the Colonial Office. His insistence is somewhat peculiar. He says plainly to the Colonial Office : You are too slow. You do not realise what chances you have lost. Even now you do not know what you can do. There is work before you. You can transform West Africa into another Egypt. There you are masters in fact. Here you have the shadow, not the substance. Nay. It is even possible in West Africa to reach the level in South Africa. There you have real control. It is possible to command it even throughout the West. We say, it is easy to kill her soul to save her life. And it is safe to remember that the soul of a people is their way of life.

Mr. Morel has written a good deal upon this West African land question. He has written with particular stress upon the Gold Coast aspect of it. The

Gold Coast bears its name well. It is about the richest gold area in the world. Its agricultural possibilities are also great. "E.D.M." is never tired of holding up to the wonder of the world her enormous cocoa developments. To quote his own words, "The chief feature in the Gold Coast report for last year, now issued, is the phenomenal increase in the export of cocoa, which rose from 50,692,949 lbs., valued at £866,571 in 1910, to 88,987,324 lbs., valued at £1,613,468 last year—an increase in value of £746,897. This agricultural feat, by native farmers, without the assistance of European capital, is so remarkable that one cannot fail to be struck with the paucity of information which the Gold Coast Administration appears to possess, or appears, at any rate, inclined to communicate with regard to it" (the *African Mail*, September 27th, 1912). There is this also which is remarkable : that it does not strike "E.D.M." that it may be a wise policy to let well alone. Crown Colonies are burdened with a curse. It is the curse of experimenting. Anyone with a patent may try his hand at it. Party politics may affect the question. Permanent officials may influence it. But the quack of all is the wire-puller —the man who knows all about it. To hold a brief for two contending views is obviously a difficult task. It is like trying to please two mistresses. Mr. Morel thinks he can do it. It is simple according to him. That is the very reason he has lost the confidence of West Africa. We are sorry to have to differ on the present occasion from an old friend. But it is just because he has been a friend that we have felt it our duty to state our convictions with candour, since a house divided against itself cannot stand. It is also in the hope that when the other side of the case has been stated, there may be a possibility of his regarding that other point of view with some tolerance, if not appreciation, and thereby help to restore the confidence of West Africa in him.

CHAPTER II.

BRITISH RELATIONS WITH WEST AFRICA.

Years ago the present writer foreshadowed in " Gold Coast Native Institutions " the possibility of a healthy imperial policy for the Gold Coast and Ashanti. To-day he ventures the same dream in regard to United West Africa. In 1903 United Nigeria had not been thought of. What is there to prevent United West Africa of the near future? It may seem presumptuous for an African to have any views upon the matter. It may appear more so to advance them. People in West Africa are supposed not to bother with such things. They are mere clay in the hands of the potter. It is not for them to indicate the " true temper of Empire." If so, we must attempt to lift the veil. We in West Africa are ardent imperialists. But our imperialism is tempered with common sense. There is a philosophy which shouts " Rule Britannia " until it is hoarse, without advancing the Empire one whit. There are conditions which apparently make for progress, but which really do retard it. It is easy to find examples even in West African history. Years ago, when a hut tax was proposed in the Sierra Leone hinterland, men pricked their ears. It was an ambitious scheme. It was an act of dominion calculated to impress outsiders. It would also impress those immediately concerned. Some sagacious ones shook their heads. Sir David Chalmers condemned the policy. He died without advancement, without recognition. The late Miss Kingsley also condemned it. She needed neither advancement nor recognition. Reproaches

did not touch her. And yet both were persons great
in their line. The prophets speak. Men heed not;
or it may be when it is too late.

Sierra Leone, we know, was founded about the
year 1787. It was a philanthropic enterprise. It
was due to the zeal of such great men as Granville
Sharp, Wilberforce, and others. The direct object
was to bring civilisation into Africa. It was not a
time for discrimination. No enquiry seems to have
been necessary as to the type of civilisation that was
desirable. Neither science, forethought, nor expe-
diency had room in the scheme of things. Right in
the heart of Africa they proceeded to erect glass
houses. They were hermetically sealed. Carefully
were the plants laid out. They were labelled as in a
museum. They were encouraged to grow. In vain
did Nature suggest fresh air and sunshine and refreshing showers. In vain was the hint that here
was opportunity to grow lilies of the valley; such
lilies, too, as might favourably compare with the
glory of a Solomon. Was it a mistake, or was it of
set purpose? Was it considered advisable that
Africans in Africa should be kept apart from their
brethren? Were they intended for a peculiar people
among their own kith and kin? If so, the scheme has
worked admirably, and Nature is revenged. Herein
is an anomaly accounted for. For, to-day, there is
a Sierra Leone Colony as distinct from the Sierra
Leone Protectorate. There is no fear of the two ever
coming together. Care has been taken that that
shall not be. It is easy to see how it has been done.
A gulf, as insuperable as that between lost souls and
the blessed in Milton's dream, is fixed. An educated
Colonist dare not openly advocate the cause of a
Protectorate chief in Sierra Leone. Alas for education! Alas, also, for the introduction of civilisation
into Africa! Philanthropy looks on this thing with
folded arms, or does not understand the treatment

of this particular phenomenon. Thinking West Africans, however, do. We have taken a favourable view of the attitude of philanthropy. But is it fair to indulge philanthropy? For we find that, in its name, the principle of isolation is proceeding in other parts of West Africa. It seems to be part of British policy to sever the educated African from the uneducated, as the sheep are severed from the goats in the parable. It is preached by faddists, by Commissioners of Districts, Commissioners of Provinces, and even by Governors. Successful advocacy leads to preferment. The advanced one is supposed to have acquired proficiency in the art of managing the " Native." False security this. Subtle influence which must evaporate as mist before the noon-day sun. Is not this a building in the sand? What sensible people ever forsook their natural leaders at the bidding of an alien power? And there are sensible folk in West Africa. Greater the seduction, greater must the reaction be. And he is not a practical man who does not see that West Africa already resents this setting of class against class. But we have digressed. We were dealing immediately with Sierra Leone and the good men who founded it. They were also great men. It was not their purpose to produce the anomaly discussed. But the policy to-day, which keeps African peoples apart; which divides that it may rule; which sows the seeds of disruption that it may reap easy dominion; that policy is not righteous, and is of set purpose.

2.

On what lines is Great Britain proceeding in West Africa? Amalgamated Nigeria might outshine India in imperial possibilities. What, then, of united West Africa? Will it be a West African Empire of

the Roman sort with the seeds of disruption in it, or
will it be one with an element of permanence? Nar-
row-minded imperialists may at once discard from
their calculations the possibility of forever keeping
the educated and the uneducated African apart. It
is a false, insidious policy. It will go the way of all
things false and insidious. According to a wise class
of thinkers, it is well that the ruled should have the
opportunity of letting the rulers know what they
think and feel. It is a natural safety-valve. All
history teaches that, where such safety-valve is not
allowed free play, the political machinery has always
toppled over. To think requires brains. Brains
move easiest when oiled by knowledge. Who is
there so base as can deny the African knowledge?
What power on earth can arrest its progress among
these people? From this it follows that just as knowledge, through the Romans, came to Britain and
stayed, so has it, through Britons, come to Africa to
stay. And, indeed, why not? It first went from
Africa to bless other lands. Africa, then, has come
unto her own, and her seers and prophets will dream
dreams of a civilisation which will have a permanence
in it.

But, to return to the argument, will British policy
in West Africa be one of repression, or one that will
give free scope to the individuality of the people? It
is possible to adopt the worse aspect of British relations with West Africa and attempt to exercise
dominion by force. That will be the way of madness.
We feel nothing but pity for some otherwise enlightened men who suggest that France and Germany,
giving less scope in their Colonies, Great Britain
should follow suit. Britain would not be Britain, if
she were France. We believe in British Imperial
West Africa. And it is just because she is neither
France nor Germany. We understand British traditions. We know them to be honourable. They are

based on fair-play. We hope to prove them so. We have no first-hand acquaintance with the traditions of other countries. We know that Britain believes in equal opportunities for all. We know that she is capable of appreciating merit and true manhood apart from the colour of a man's skin, or the circumstances of his birth. We know, too, unfortunately, that Britain is human, after all, and sometimes requires the grace of God to keep true to her high ideals.

It is also possible for Great Britain to stand by her treaty rights in West Africa and say, I will enforce the contract. That would be indiscreet. You may enforce a contract with an individual. You cannot enforce a contract with a whole people except at the point of the bayonet. So the second course would be the same as the first, and as bad. In Nigeria, as in Sierra Leone, remember, your primary object was trade. Trade with the interior was considered the way to bring them civilisation. It is conceivable that neither by conquest, nor cession, can all Nigeria be claimed. There are cases where the reversion may be traced to native landowners. The Royal Niger Company were honest people. They fought only where it was absolutely necessary. They generally respected the rights of the people. Hence the hold they had on them. We know that the officials of the Royal Niger Company refrained from giving evidence before the Nigerian Land Committee. We should so like to know their idea as to the nature of their own relationship to the Nigerians. We know for a fact this much, that the land question has aroused all West Africa. Our Southern Nigerian friends have raised the question of the alleged cession, and are prepared to test it. And the facts are so interesting that we must state them in the course of this paper with the law bearing upon them.

3.

It appears that in April, 1911, the community of Lagos were considerably alarmed by the judgment of the Full Court in what is known as " The Foreshore Case." The said judgment affirmed the finding of the Court Below, that " Lagos land was the property of King Docemo." From this the Crown appears to have taken up the position that King Docemo, having in August, 1861, ceded the port and island of Lagos to the British Government, such cession had passed the property in the land to the Government. It is suggested that such finding was not necessary to the immediate issue before the Court, and that it was, in a sense, an *obiter dictum*.

Anyway, it was useful in that it called for an authoritative examination of the facts, and a clear statement of them in the able speech of a leading member of the deputation which waited upon the Acting Governor of Southern Nigeria on the Lagos Land question, to which we are indebted for this summary. The whole speech is well worth reading and preserving. The calm logic of it is bound to appeal to you. And if you take interest in West African manhood and nationality, you cannot help taking courage that if, so far, West Africa has produced politicians of the type of Mr. Edum and others, her future is in safe hands.

Now for the facts. It seems that about the time of the cession Her Majesty's Government were anxious to put an end to the slave trade in Lagos and the neighbouring countries, and thought it desirable to secure the island and port of Lagos as a suitable ground for operations. What was aimed at, as disclosed by the terms of cession and the correspondence, was "the establishment of British sovereignty" at Lagos. It was neither contemplated, nor understood, that the treaty involved forfeiture of private rights of ownership. And, indeed, the judgment of the Full Court had expressly stated that the cession of August, 1861, was a cession of all lands "not subject to pre-existing rights of private ownership." The actual words of the learned Chief Justice were : "It seems to me to be quite clear that the treaty of 1861 was a cession of territory, which at the same time respected pre-existing rights of private ownership."

From this it becomes of considerable importance to inquire whether at the time of the cession there were any lands "not subject to pre-existing rights of private ownership"; what rights passed under the cession to the Crown; and the practical effect, in the light of the facts, of the judgment of the Full Court.

In Lagos, there are Chiefs known as the "White Cap Chiefs." These, the speaker proves clearly, are the "Civil Lords" whose consent and concurrence in any grant of lands were necessary to make such grant valid. The four Councillors who signed the articles of cession did not belong to the class of "White Cap Chiefs." They were mere officers of the Crown, and formed the King's Council. In the treaty we read the words : "I, Docemo, do with the consent and advice of my Council." Here comes in the confusion of European ideas with African principles of land tenure. If the ultimate ownership of the lands, as in England, was in the King, Docemo's grant would pass the lands. But if, *qua* King, he did not own the lands, but they were subject to pre-existing rights of private ownership, obviously they did not, and could not, pass under the grant. To set this point at rest, a declaration of the Under Secretary of State for Foreign Affairs in the House of Commons on June 12th, 1862, is quoted. He said : "My right

honourable friend was in error when he talked of the
land belonging to Docemo; the real possessors of it
were certain White Cap Chiefs, as they were called.
When the deed of cession was proposed to Docemo,
a fear arose among the White Cap Chiefs lest they
were to be deprived of their rights, but their appre-
hensions were soon set at rest, and Docemo himself
was fully satisfied when he found that a yearly
revenue was to be guaranteed to him on the faith of
a treaty." If, then, the land did not belong to King
Docemo, and in the case in which the Full Court's
judgment was recorded the real owners of the lands
were not parties thereto, and it can be shown
that there is not an inch of soil in Lagos not subject
to pre-existing rights of private ownership, the judgment in question stands stripped of any value, and,
at best, can be regarded as a harmless *obiter dictum.*

Nor can one possibly reconcile the attitude of the
Government in September, 1911, when it sought to
take advantage of the Full Court's judgment, and its
own acts and judgments in the past. It is shown that
after the treaty of cession the Government, wanting
land for public purposes, acquired it from persons
having pre-existing rights of private ownership under
the " Public Lands Ordinance, No. 8 of 1876."   It
is pointed out that this Ordinance distinctly recognises that there are no " waste lands."   As to judgments, the Supreme Court records are quoted to show
that His Majesty's Judges had, from time to time,
determined and upheld private rights of ownership
claimed under " pre-existing rights."

A remarkable debate in the Legislative Council of
Lagos on July 1st, 1908, led by the Honourable
Sapara Williams, the able leader of the Lagos Bar,
with respect to the " Ikoyi Lands Ordinance, 1908,"
took place. Said he :—

" Whereas by a treaty dated August 6th, 1861,

" Docemo, King of Lagos, on the part of himself and
" Chiefs, gave and transferred unto the Queen of Great
" Britain, her heirs and successors for ever, the port and
" Island of Lagos, with all the rights, profits, territories
" and appurtenances whatsoever thereunto belonging:
" and whereas the said Island of Lagos is now divided
" into unequal portions by the cutting known as McGregor
" Canal: and whereas the greater part of the portion
" situate to the east of that canal (generally known as
" Ikoyi) is still Crown land, never having been alienated
" to private owners.''

" As a matter of fact Docemo never ceded this place
" to the British Government; he had not got it to cede.
" He ceded at the time what he had the right to give
" away, namely, his sovereign rights. Long anterior to
" his accession to the throne, as far back as the time of
" Addo, the first King of Lagos, Ikoyi was in the occupa-
" tion of Chief Onikoyi, who was there exercising the
" right acknowledged by all the Kings of Lagos.   Kings
" of Lagos never could grant lands to strangers, because
" they had none to give. If a stranger wanted land, and
" approached the King, the King sends to the Chief of the
" district in which the particular land is situate, and the
" Chief is the person who allots the land to the stranger,
" and receives from him the customary presents for the
" permission to occupy for his own use. To show that
" this is so, Captain Glover, during his Governorship,
" applied to the then Onikoyi for a grant of this land for
" the purpose of allotting it to the Hausas who had been
" discharged from the Force for agricultural purposes.
" The Onikoyi went with Captain Glover over the land,
" and pointed out to him the boundary. This land was
" granted to Captain Glover as the representative of the
" British Crown. Furthermore, Docemo was living then,
" and if it was understood at the time, or if Captain
" Glover, who assumed the reins of Government so close
" upon the treaty of cession, and who would assuredly
" have known, was of opinion even that this land was
" ceded under the treaty he would never have applied to
" the Onikoyi in this matter for the grant thereof, but
" would have taken it as of right. Governor Glover came
" here in 1864 and went away in 1872. The transaction
" shows that the Crown admitted the rights of the
" Onikoyi and recognised them. The Government
" accepted the land on behalf of Her Majesty, her heirs

" and successors. The preamble is not set out correctly ; it
" is incomplete with regard to the terms under which
" you are holding the land at Ikoyi. There was a judg-
" ment relating to this land in the case of Aluko Onikoyi
" versus Jimba, which was published in the Gazette
" about two years ago."

The learned Attorney General acquiesced in the
contention of the Honourable Member in these
words :

" I agree with the Honourable Member that the
" preamble is misleading, because it conveys the idea that
" the fee simple of the whole of this land was granted by
" King Docemo to the Crown. That is not the case, and
" it is inconsistent with the judgment, I understand,
" that was given by Chief Justice Nicoll, which estab-
" lished the fact that a large portion of Ikoyi was granted
" to the Queen by the Chief who was mentioned by the
" Honourable Member. I quite agree with the Honour-
" able Member that some alteration of the preamble is
" absolutely necessary. Therefore I am quite ready to
" agree to its amendment."

Accordingly, the following amendments were
made :—

" The first part of the preamble is amended by insert-
" ing after the word ' ever ' ' his sovereign rights over.'
" The third part of the preamble is amended by insert-
" ing after the word 'whereas,' ' the fee simple in posses-
" sion of ' and by deleting the words ' is still Crown land,
" never having been alienated to private owners,' and
" then substituting the words ' was granted to the British
" Crown in or about the year 1865,' which fact was estab-
" lished by a judgment of the Supreme Court of the
" Colony in the year 1904."

This summary may usefully close with the Report
of His Honour Chief Justice T. C. Rayner, now Chief
Justice of British Guiana, and Mr. John J. C. Healey,
Commissioner of Lands, upon Land Tenure in West
Africa. Wrote the learned Chief Justice :—

" ' All land in West Africa, though apparently unoccu-
" pied, has an owner;' ' and then,' it is said, ' he con-
" tinues to deal with the rights of native ownership,

" alienation, sale, introduction of English ideas, in-
" heritance, cause of confusion by Crown Grants, culti-
" vation, and pledging.' "

" Mr. Healey confines himself to Land Tenure in
" Lagos. He states the conditions under which land is
" given or allotted according to native Tenure, and
" describes the manner in which land was dealt with in
" Lagos between 1854 and 1897, within various periods."

It is unfortunate that in the year 1912 the Government of Southern Nigeria should seek to put an in-
terpretation upon King Docemo's treaty cession not
justified by the facts. We own the temptation was
sore, and one hard to resist. The pressure from
within and without was great. Certain Socialist
members of the House of Commons had urged
uniform Government land control in West Africa.
At last the Colonial Office had come to believe in it.
It was openly said that the Department felt some sort
of action imperative. Pious things were uttered.
When the scramble for Africa began, then also men
uttered pious words. But not all pious utterances
are true. The pity of it is that those who uttered
them knew them to be untrue. It was to save the
soul of Africa. It was to rescue her from degradation. These saviours were the vice-gerents of the
Highest—the Trustees of the helpless. We know
what happened at the Congo. We know what may
happen when once the " pre-existing rights of private
ownership " pass over to the Government in West
Africa. Hence the diffidence of the people. Who
can honestly blame them?

4.

Again, take Yorubaland in Southern Nigeria.
There the Alake is master in theory and in fact. He
is a full-blown ruler under British protection. He is
the medium of British authority. It may, or may not
be, an eyesore to the local Administration. We say
local advisedly. For Colonial Office policy, as defined in after-dinner speeches, does not always find

favour in local official circles.   All the same, public
notices in Yorubaland are signed by the Alake and
his Secretary.   This is defined in diplomatic circles
as the method of " indirect rule."   " Indirect rule "
is, apparently, favoured by Mr. Morel.   That is suggested in his new work on " Nigeria : Its Peoples and
its Problems."   But petty officers sometimes find it
irksome.   They would curb it, or end it.   Even Mr.
Morel has suggested that if the British Government
liked it could end the situation.   But that, of course,
was in dealing with the land.   The land question is a
sore point.   It affords endless temptation.   Its syren
voice can carry away even heaven-born philanthropists.   If " indirect rule " will not pair with it,
" indirect rule " must go.   Of course, it means this :
Given the ultimate control of the lands in the Government, with a declaration of mere user in the people,
the Chief may have as much direct rule as he likes.
Can British policy stand the strain when West African
opinion presses for the substance rather than the
shadow?   That must come.   That will be the dividing line between the class of politicians represented
by Mr. Morel and enlightened West African opinion
which they affect to despise.

Mr. Morel is fascinated with the Northern Nigeria
Lands Proclamation.   He is for ever singing its
praises.   But it is essentially an act of dominion.   It
may, or may not, be justified.   It may, or may not,
work well.   But that is no reason why it should be
thrust upon other communities.   Of course, Mr.
Morel is anxious that British dominion should be
universal in West Africa.   And he has one patent
for it.   He can conceive of none other.   He recks
not what the facts are.   When you point out to him
that the Gold Coast was never acquired by conquest,
cession, or purchase, he retorts, who talked of conquest?   Occasionally, however, he is forced to admit

that the situation is a decidedly delicate one. The responsible Ministers of the Crown also appreciate this. Mr. Harcourt's speech in Parliament, reported in the *Times* of June 28th, 1912, is significant of much : " After referring to the land system initiated in Northern Nigeria by Sir Frederick Lugard, he expressed the opinion that however excellent a land system might be as applied to a new country, it was not always possible to apply it to other territories which had already adopted and developed a land system on different lines. He did not wish to argue that land reform was impossible in any country, however highly organised or conservative in its customs, but the pace ought to vary with the circumstances of the case and the inertia or toleration of the people."

Sir Charles Bruce has told us that : " In the Crown Colonies all legislation is liable to be amended, modified or reversed to meet the exigencies of party politics in the Imperial Parliament." In a moment of irritation, Mr. Morel threatened in the columns of the *African Mail* to uphold his West African land policy in the Press, on the platform, and in Parliament. Now that he is likely to get there, men are wondering whether he can conscientiously deny the wisdom and the justice of the Colonial Minister's authoritative pronouncement. We have directed attention to his suggestion that if the British Government liked it could end the situation. True. But is it advisable? Is there no other way? We know there is. We say that it is even possible to realise Mr. Morel's dream of a Yoruba National Council without vesting Yoruba lands in Government as trustees or otherwise. We say that the insisting upon the indigenes' right of user merely in terms of the Northern Nigeria Lands Proclamation is tantamount to an act of confiscation. It is sought to extend this proclamation to Southern Nigeria, to Sierra Leone,

and to the Gold Coast. We say that this from even
our best friends must give us pause. Empire building in West Africa, raised upon the ashes of the
peoples' proprietary rights, is raised in sand. We
admit that the argument, as advanced, is subtle. It
is possible to take in the unwary. A little scrutiny,
however, makes it all clear. It shows that in this
deal, on the plea of protecting native interests, the
protectors will come off top best. And it is more
than likely that enlightened West Africa will use
every constitutional means to make itself heard and
understood.

And yet the people of West Africa are the easiest
ruled within the British Dominions. Only their sense
of justice must be respected. And whether you
claim by conquest or cession, unless proprietary
rights are sympathetically adjusted, we fear there
will be trouble. Such sympathetic treatment with
regard to Ashanti is suggested in Mr. Belfield's report
on Gold Coast Land Tenure. He lays it down clearly
that " the claim to ownership which might have been
enforced at the time of occupation was waived, and
cannot now be asserted." And it was a wise policy
which dictated non-assertion. What good purpose
would it have served, if dominion had been asserted
and enforced? What is it that Britain wants in West
Africa? Is it a huge, unwieldy territory under military surveillance, or free friendly States or Dependencies pouring into the lap of Britannia the rich
products of their lands? Study the situation.
Examine the actual facts. Here is a country where
a European cannot rear a family; whose economic
developments are endless; whose potentialities are
enormous. The inhabitants thereof are, obviously,
of more value than all the gold embedded in the soil,
or all the economic products that can be turned out.
For, without them, neither the one nor the other is
possible. Which is of more value, theoretical occupa-

tion, or the hearts of the people; aggressive dominion
or sympathetic treatment? You have hitherto taxed
them without representation; you have practically
closed the door to equal opportunity against them;
you have succumbed on occasion to the temptation
of insisting upon invidious distinctions; you have
often yielded to prejudice. All this they have borne
with a patience which is characteristic. But in this
land question they have spoken plainly. They will
not give them up under any pretext whatever. And
they have sufficient intelligence to discriminate
between the inroads of capital and the aggression of
the Protector.

There is, after all, a small difference between us
and Mr. Morel. But it is a radical difference. He
offers us *pax Britannica* in exchange for our lands;
" indirect rule " in exchange for Government land
control. " Indirect rule " is good. But it, with
mere user of land, is bad. West Africa will have
none of it.

CHAPTER III.

BRITISH RELATIONS WITH THE GOLD COAST.

The Gold Coast is not another India. Yet is there much that is in common in the history of the two Dependencies worthy of the study of the political student and the guidance of the practical statesman.

India's dilemma was Great Britain's opportunity. The internal strife of its princes made it possible for the East India Company to gain influence. They gradually came to interfere in the affairs of the people. The Crown did not encourage this at first. Legislative sanction was given afterwards. Then came developments which led to regular administration by Her Majesty's Government. Later, we have the Indian Mutiny, the result, among other causes, of the rulers not sufficiently appreciating the prejudices of the ruled. This led to a new policy, which, under the guiding spirit of the Queen's proclamations, made it possible for India, in time, in some modified form, to take a part in the management of her internal affairs. It was felt that it was impossible in a Dependency where the proportion of the rulers to the ruled was four to one million not to take note and give effect to the people's point of view. It was realised that in dealing with even an Eastern people fair-play was in the end the only goal at which practical statesmen could aim. It was recognised by such a distinguished administrator as Sir Thomas Munro that of the three policies of plunder, servitude, or amalgamation, the soundest and safest was the last. How could Great Britain perpetually overawe or enslave

such a virile, ancient race as the Indians? No. A
policy of conciliation, of amalgamation, was the only
one possible. Sir Thomas Munro, we are told by Sir
Charles Bruce in his able work, " The True Temper
of Empire," advocated the one possible policy. Said
he :

> " Let Britain be subjugated by a foreign Power to-
> " morrow ; let the people be excluded from all share in
> "the Government, from public honour, from every
> " office of high trust or emolument, and let them, in
> " every situation, be considered as unworthy of trust,
> " and all their knowledge, and all their literature, sacred
> " and profane, would not save them from becoming, in
> " another generation or two, a low-minded, deceitful, and
> " dishonest race."

The Government of India, then, was to be based
on the confidence, the consent, and the co-operation
of the people of India. Thus, we find a large portion of the country being governed through the
agency of feudatory Chiefs, the interests of India,
theoretically or practically, being the first consideration of the Government, the same being made to
harmonise with the interests of the Crown.

The trend of events in the Gold Coast did not
exactly run that way. True, there was the " African
Company of Merchants," constituted by Act of Parliament, with liberty to trade and form establishments
on the West Coast of Africa, between 20 degrees N.
and 20 degrees S. lat. Under the able administration
of Governor Maclean, the Company had gained considerable influence ever the Chiefs of the country.
But there were no internal dissensions of any importance. The sole trouble arose from Ashanti. The
Company's servants, and subsequently the Government, found cause to embroil themselves in Ashanti
affairs. It culminated in the defeat and death of Sir
Charles Macarthy in 1824 at the battle of Insimakaw.
The bearing of Ashanti affairs upon the British posi-

tion on the Gold Coast has been carefully traced in
" Gold Coast Native Institutions," pages 151 to 158,
which may be referred to with advantage. At no
time was it claimed that British participation in these
disputes gave Her Majesty's Government any addi-
tional jurisdiction than that which had been conferred
by the Bond of 1844, or such civil jurisdiction which
was exercised by the tacit acquiescence of the people.
Indeed, Sir Frederick Hodgson, in introducing the
Estimates, said :

> " I do not, I may state, regard Ashanti as being in the
> " same position to the Government as other districts
> " which together form the colony and protected terri-
> " tories of the Gold Coast. Ashanti is a conquered coun-
> " try—a country upon which blood and treasure have
> " been spent—and the kings and chiefs know that in
> " accordance with native custom they must pay tribute
> " to the paramount authority."

In " Fanti Customary Laws," the able work of my
late learned friend the Honourable J. Mensah Sarbah,
C.M.G., Senior Unofficial Member of the Legislative
Council, it is written :

> " The King, by the Law of England, is the Supreme
> " Lord of the whole soil.   Whoever, therefore, holds
> " lands must hold them mediately or immediately from
> " him ; and while the subject enjoys usufructuary posses-
> " sion, the absolute and ultimate dominion remains in
> " the King.

> " As far as the Gold Coast is concerned, this portion
> " of the English Law does not apply, for it is a group of
> " territories under native rulers taken under British pro-
> " tection. It is British territory, but not so by conquest
> " or cession. As a matter of fact the Colonial Office
> " stated on March 11th, 1887, as published in a Parlia-
> " mentary Blue Book of that year, that it is inaccurate
> " to state that after the successful Ashanti Expedition of
> " 1874, the Protectorate was annexed by Great Britain
> " and became a Colony, inasmuch as the greater portion
> " of the Gold Coast Colony still remains a Protectorate,
> " the soil being in the hands of the natives and under the
> " jurisdiction of Native Chiefs.

" According to native ideas there is no land without
" owners. What is a now a forest or unused land will, as
" years go on, come under cultivation by subjects of the
" Stool or members of the village community, or other
" members of the community."

Mr. W. H. Adams, B.A., B.L., a District Commissioner of the Gold Coast, in Government *Gazette*
Extraordinary of August 13th, 1897, wrote :

" Every acre of land on the Gold Coast has an owner.
" There is no unoccupied land. Though no boundaries
" may be visible to the European, they are perfectly clear
" to the eyes of the owners. It would seem as if in the
" remote past the whole land has been vested in the
" various Kings, each Stool, with its boundaries, forming
" a commonwealth."

It is a curious fact that Her Majesty's jurisdiction
in criminal matters on the Gold Coast originated with
the Bond of 1844. As a side-light upon this, the
despatch of the Committee of the African Merchants,
then administering the forts and settlements under
the Crown, dated October 20, 1836, is of considerable importance. It shows what the position was
before the Bond in question. The despatch ran as
follows :

" Your proceedings in Council, April 6th, in reference
" to the trials of Adoasi and Ammah for wilful murder,
" we observe, were conducted in the Public Hall of Cape
" Coast in your presence and that of Cabboceers and
" Peynins, and, found guilty upon their own confession,
" these men were executed. It seems, from your in-
" formation to us, that there has been a very important
" departure from the proceedings of our Criminal Courts,
" inasmuch as the confession of the prisoners was the
" chief evidence against them, but of the justice of the
" sentence there can be no doubt. These remarks lead
" us to remark to you, which we feel bound to do, that
" we have been instructed expressly by Lord Cleneg ' that
" the British Government pretends neither to territorial
" possession, nor to jurisdiction over any portion of the
" Gold Coast, excepting the actual site of the several
" forts and castles.' It is, therefore, necessary that your
" authority should be exercised with very great caution."

Even after the Bond the Secretary of State on November 23rd, 1865, found it necessary to write as follows with respect to assumed jurisdiction :—

" Sir,—I have to acknowledge your despatch No. 144
" of 17th October, enclosing the copy of a notice which
" you have issued, in which you define the limits of Her
" Majesty's possessions on the Gold Coast. I am unable
" to approve the step which you have taken in declaring
" the territory within five miles of eight separate British
" forts to be British territory, and I have to instruct you
" to recall the notices in which this is done. Whatever
" influence you may be able to exert in discouraging or
" repressing barbarous customs leading to loss of life will
" be very proper, and I shall be happy to approve your
" exercise of it, but the extension of British territory is
" a different matter, and cannot receive my sanction."

Again, on the 22nd of December of the same year, the Secretary writes to the Lieutenant-Governor " to " avoid introducing any expressions which bear the " appearance of extending jurisdiction over territory " at the Gold Coast "; and on the 23rd of December he once more urges upon him " to avoid any new step " which may have that appearance."

Indeed, so clear was the understanding as to the Queen's jurisdiction on the Gold Coast that Colonel Ord, giving evidence before the Select Committee appointed in the sixties to ascertain the relations between the Gold Coast and Great Britain, stated that he conceived that if any tax on the people was to be carried out, it could only be effected " with the consent and the direct co-operation of the Chiefs themselves."

Thus, in a different way, we came to the same situation in the Gold Coast as in India. There, as here, the rule of the people is based on their confidence, consent, and co-operation. And it is significant of much that the opening message of His Excellency Sir Hugh Clifford, the present enlightened Governor of the Gold Coast, is for frank co-operation

on the part of the Chiefs and people. We are glad
to be able to think that this is also the policy of the
Colonial Office, as exemplified by the circular letter
to the Chiefs, dated 9th January, 1913, which ran as
follows :—

> " The Secretary of State is anxious to secure the co-
> " operation of the Head Chiefs and Chiefs in all matters
> " which affect the welfare of the Colony and its in-
> " habitants, and that this Government will always be
> " pleased to receive and consider their views with regard
> " to legislative measures or matters of administration."

It is noteworthy that this circular letter was issued
after the people's petition to His Majesty the King in
Council in August, 1912, praying for fuller representation in the Legislative Council and representation on
the Executive Council, which petition was presented
on behalf of the deputation by Messrs. Ashurst,
Morris, Crisp & Co., after the same had been settled
by Mr. Tim Healy, K.C., M.P.

On the Gold Coast there has never been another
Indian Mutiny. Tact, prudence and loyalty have been
the leading traits of her sons. But they have been
firm in their protests against encroachments on their
rights when the necessity has arisen. The lands are in
the hands of family groups in distinct chieftainships;
and there is no legal conception clearer than the distinction between ownership and paramountcy, which
later will be noticed.

2.

It may not be generally known that the Gold Coast,
unlike Northern Nigeria, or even Ashanti, has never
been acquired by Great Britain either by conquest,
cession, or purchase. In fact, so well is this fact
recognised that the Attorney-General of the Gold
Coast in February, 1911, stated : " I am of the
opinion that no land in the Colony other than the
forts and their immediate surroundings, and such
land as has from time to time been acquired by the

Government for specific public purposes, can be considered to be Crown Land. I acquiesce in the opinion that all land in the Colony is owned by someone.''

It is important to explain that this view as to the ownership of the soil of the Gold Coast being in the indigenes had not always been common in Government circles, and that it was not until after strenuous effort and careful explanation on the part of the people that acquiescense in the proposition by the local authorities, at the least, was obtained. For we know that in the year 1894 the '' Crown Lands Bill '' was introduced by the local Legislature with the intention of vesting the lands of the country in the Crown. This was opposed by the people, and, upon criticism, was abandoned by the direction of Her Majesty's Secretary of State to the Colonies. Again, in 1897, a similar attempt was made, this time to administer the lands of the people, on the plea that timber was recklessly felled and improvident alienations made. A deputation to Downing Street on this occasion was sent by the people, and, after having been accorded a reception by the Right Honourable Joseph Chamberlain, M.P., the then Colonial Minister, he admitted that the objections to the measure were valid, and, in the result, directed a merely regulative measure to be passed in the shape of the '' Concessions Ordinance, 1900,'' under which grants of land have since been made. In the petition of the people they had urged that the Supreme Court of the Gold Coast should be the authority to decide as to the validity of grants and, after mature consideration, the reasonableness of the suggestion had appealed to Mr. Chamberlain. For, from the beginning of the relations between Great Britain and the Gold Coast, confidence had been inspired in the breasts of the people by reason of the steady application of the principles of fair play, justice, and equity which Her Majesty's Judges, then known as judicial assesors to the Native Rulers, had brought to bear upon matters which came before them, either as between individuals, or as between the Government and the people. In fact, so deep-rooted has been such confidence that the present writer found it possible, as far back as 1903, to write in " Gold Coast Native Institutions " (London : Sweet and Maxwell, Ltd.) at page 220, thus :—

" Strange as it may seem, they serve Great Britain " best who serve her in truth and godly fear. Men like " Sir David Chalmers, Chief Justice Macleod, and others " of like grit, who looked not to promotion or official " applause in the manly discharge of their simple duty, " are the ones who dig deep the foundations of British " Supremacy in West Africa.   For, believe me, the "Native of West Africa has profound respect for the " qualities of justice and fair-play. The careless observer " may think that the fear of British guns and Maxims " has hitherto kept the Gold Coast proper free from dis-"turbances. A greater mistake could not be made. If " you want to know what has hitherto been a tower of " strength to the British Government on the Gold Coast, " you will find it in the confidence which has been in-" spired in the native mind by the Judges of the Supreme " Court, who have been, taking them generally, men of " singular uprightness, fairness and ability, independent " of bureaucratic influence. But they have not worked " alone. They have been supported by a strong and loyal " Bar, a band of men in whom the clients have the most " implicit confidence, and who generally succeed in " throwing the oil of peace upon the troubled waters of " popular passion and ferment. They help to make the " administration of the country possible ; ' but the figure-" heads generally receive all the praise, and the lawyers " all the opprobrium.'

" You have only to suggest to a native chief, smarting " under a sense of wrong, real or imaginary, that the " Court will look into his case, and he will patiently bide " his time for months till the whole matter has been " thrashed out. If he is defeated, he will retire with " good grace from the scene of conflict, and all because " he has implicit confidence in both Bench and Bar. " What honest man is there, I ask with all seriousness,

" who will dare to shake such confidence? It will be an
" evil day for the Gold Coast when the native client
" begins to lose confidence in either Bench or Bar. It
" will be but the beginning of the end, with chaos and
" black ruin attending it, of which, happily, I see no sign
" at present."

But to return to the history of land legislation on
the Gold Coast, the 1897 attempt having failed, in
1910 a "Forest Ordinance" was introduced in the
local Legislature which sought to vest the lands of the
people in the Crown by compulsory acquisition. Upon
criticism by counsel on behalf of the people in the
Legislative Council, compulsory acquisition was
dropped in favour of the taking up of leaseholds by
Government. It was seriously suggested that Government should transform itself into a huge corpora-
tion for the purpose of acquiring and managing the
lands of the people. This proposition was equally
stoutly opposed by the people, who sent a second
deputation to Downing Street, gently but firmly to
remind the Colonial Minister that by the pledge given
by Mr. Chamberlain in 1898 the land question of the
Gold Coast was settled once and for all; that the
understanding then come to had since been regarded
by the people as their Magna Charter; and that the
situation urged by Mr. Morel, the able Editor of the
African Mail, and those who are of his way of thinking, was easily capable of exaggeration.

But how came Mr. Morel to be so intimately connected with this question? How came he to have
threatened in his paper that certain reforms, in his
view, being necessary, he would leave no stone un-
turned through the Press, on the platform, and in
Parliament, to force home his ideas as to land reform
in the Gold Coast? Mark you, Mr. Morel has never
been to the Gold Coast, nor has he ever been known
to lay claim to any exceptional knowledge of Native
Law and custom, or the institutions of the people.

All these are intricate subjects, often requiring deep study on the part of jurists and others to grasp fully. Yet has Mr. Morel found it possible, while taking no notice of the people's point of view as to his suggested land reform, to charge their leaders with folly in attempting to show that there are two sides to every question. It will repay the reader, who desires to comprehend the whole question, to study the two pamphlets which have been issued by the present writer on "Gold Coast Land Tenure and The Forest Bill, 1911." (London : C. M. Phillips, 14, Portugal Street.) Well, to attempt an explanation of Mr. Morel's connection with this matter, what happened was this. A few years ago articles began to appear in the *African Mail* as to an alleged improvident alienation of what is loosely called "tribal lands," and it was insisted that it was the duty of Government to step in and prevent such alienation. This, it will occur to the reader, was the old cry revived—the cry which called forth the "Lands Bill" in the time of Mr. Chamberlain's administration. Mr. Morel has claimed for himself and his friends in the columns of the *African Mail* the credit of having got the Colonial Office seriously to regard the alleged situation on the Gold Coast. He was also, in a large measure, responsible for the appointment of Mr. H. Conway Belfield, C.M.G., as Special Commissioner to the Gold Coast upon this land question, and we know that ere Mr. Belfield's report was published, he and others had waited on the Right Honourable the Secretary of State to the Colonies, urged the appointment of a Departmental Committee of the Colonial Office to enquire into this same matter, and he, Mr. Morel, had accepted a place on the Committee. All this may be gathered from recent correspondence in *The Times.*

Now, Mr. H. Conway Belfield, at one time British

Resident, Perak Federated Malay States, now Governor of British East Africa, arrived on the Gold Coast on February 16th, 1912, to prosecute inquiries into the tenure and disposition of land. He left the country on the 29th of April, arriving in London on May 14th, 1912. Considering, therefore, that the Special Commissioner's stay did not exceed two months and a half, the voluminous Report on the " Legislation Governing the Alienation of Native Lands in the Gold Coast and Ashanti, with some observations on the ' Forest Ordinance,' 1911," which now lies before us, is a marvel of industry of which any man might justly feel proud. But, all the same, when one thinks of the amount of matter he must have had to wade through, the series of papers dealing with matters of land administration which it was considered desirable by the local authorities that he should see (page 1, Cd. 6278), and the various local conditions with which he must have had to make himself familiar; it is no wonder, as the *African World* has pointed out, that the report has a strong tinge of conclusions applicable to Malay States conditions.

It would be an interesting study to discuss the points of this report, but, for the present, we must be satisfied with a few leading propositions.

The Special Commissioner, having admitted that it would be a breach of faith on the part of the British Government to attempt to exercise rights of ownership over the lands of the people, he proceeds to recommend the transference of jurisdiction in Land Grants from the Supreme Court to the Executive, reserving, however, the rights of appeal. This proposition, innocent as it may seem, will strike the thoughtful reader to go to the very root of the relations between the Government and the people. For it will be remembered that the Bond of 1844, which gave Her Majesty for the first time criminal jurisdiction in the country, was silent as to jurisdiction in civil matters, and, nothwithstanding the gradual growth of such jurisdiction with the tacit consent of the people, by the " Native Jurisdiction Ordinance of 1911 " (a merely regulative measure) the Native Tribunals have exclusive jurisdiction over land cases, the title to which is not based on written documents. It becomes obvious, therefore, what a drastic change is suggested by the transference of jurisdiction in concession cases practically from the Supreme Court to the Executive. As to this, Sir William Nevill M'Geary, in an interesting special letter to the *African World* of August 3rd, 1912, says : " Two facts must be brought home to the public, that there is a general confidence by natives and Europeans in the British Courts, and, I regret to say, a growing distrust of the British Government as exemplified in the experience of any one who has had to deal with the ' Secretariat.' " And it is worth remembering that Sir William was some time the Attorney-General of the Gold Coast, and was writing after eighteen years' experience of West Africa in general.

CHAPTER IV.

THE TRUTH ABOUT THE LAND QUESTION.

It is with some degree of reluctance that we find ourselves compelled to notice the series of articles which have appeared in the *African Mail* on the Forest Bill and upon the land question under the initials of the Editor.

" E. D. M." having admitted that he first raised the land question on the Gold Coast and forced it upon the attention of the Colonial Office and upon Parliament, one should have thought that he would have been anxious to place before the public through the columns of his paper all the information available upon the very questions raised by him from whatever source gleaned.   Instead of that, it is to be regretted, that the columns of the *African Mail* had, up to July 26, 1912, been as a sealed book to the statement of facts of those whom in his haste he had charged with folly.   He had not chosen to inform his readers that the " Forest Bill," a very substantial outcome of his representations, had contained clauses as to compulsory acquisition of the lands of the Gold Coast, and that, upon solid facts being pressed upon the notice of the local Legislature and the Colonial Office, the Government had withdrawn from the position.   In passing, the argument roundly stated was that there were no Crown lands on the Gold Coast, the country never having been acquired by conquest, cession, or purchase, and that the land question, as far as the Gold Coast was concerned, had, as long ago as the year 1898, been thrashed out, and not open to question. His Excellency the Governor, who had heard Counsel at the Legislative Council, had said :

" I am very glad to have had an opportunity of hearing
"the views of Counsel on behalf of certain native rulers of
" the country, and I congratulate them upon the clear and
" moderate manner in which they have put forward their
" arguments."

It did not occur to Mr. Morel to summarise for his readers the main arguments which had so favourably impressed the Legislative Council. It was inconvenient for him, perhaps, to inform the public that the Government had given way on the matter of compulsory acquisition. But he still found it possible to write from week to week as if nothing had happened; nor did he, even after his own views upon the " educated native " had been somewhat modified by force of circumstances, condescend to take his readers into his confidence as to the causes which had led to such modification. We regret to be compelled to think that this is not the way we expected Mr. Morel to have conducted this controversy. Hence the necessity which has arisen for a calm and a clear statement of the full facts of the situation.

In the April 12th, 1912, issue of the *African Mail* will be found Mr. Morel's article on the " Gold Coast Land Question." In that article he gives the names of those who had helped him with information and given him assistance in Parliament. Among these he mentions Mr. Josiah Wedgwood, M.P., who, he tells us, took up the matter in the Anti-Slavery Society's *Bulletin*. We take it, then, that Mr. Wedgwood was writing from information gleaned from Mr. Morel, or capable of being corrected, if wrong, by Mr. Morel. We have before us, as we write, the very issue, namely, that of July, 1911, of the *Anti-Slavery Reporter and Aborigines' Friend*, in which Mr. Wedg-

wood's article on the subject appeared. It will be
necessary for us to quote Mr. Wedgwood freely for
the reader with an unbiassed mind to see for himself
the origin of this land question, and what is aimed at
and intended by it. Says the writer under the heading " Native Lands and Crown Colonies " :—" The
intimate connection between slavery and the native
land question could not be shown more clearly than
it has been by Sir Percy Girourard. He writes : —

> " My predecessor in Northern Nigeria (Sir Frederick
> " Lugard), referring to the difficulty of obtaining free
> " labour (after the abolition of slavery), mentions the
> " necessity of the ' creation of a labouring class to till
> " the lands of the ruling classes,' and the ' enforcement
> " of proprietary rights in land ' as the solution. I can
> " only presume that this meant the creation of a landlord
> " class. I am not at all certain that it would be in the
> " natives' interest to create a landlord class."

" And in two years he took effective steps to prevent the possibility of a landlord class, black or white,
ever arising in Northern Nigeria." Here is certainly
food for thought. But let us proceed. Continuing,
Mr. Wedgwood says :—

> " Observe that the difficulty of obtaining labour came
> " from the abolition of slavery ; that, as long as the
> " natives could work for themselves on free lands, wage
> " labour was scarce and costly ; and lastly, that Sir F.
> " Lugard clearly saw that the way to get over the
> " ' difficulty ' of scarcity of labour was by depriving the
> " natives of free land. It would hardly be fair to say
> " that he *advocated* this way out of the difficulty ; indeed,
> " all his actions show he was entirely opposed to the
> " solution, but with a certain cynicism he pointed out the
> " way for those who might wish to introduce European
> " ' civilisation ' into darkest Africa. His successor
> " slammed the door in the face of ' civilisation.' One
> " wonders how long it will remain shut."

European " civilisation," then, according to this
class of thinkers, demands cheap labour. To get
cheap labour, the natives must be deprived of free

land. Indeed, Mr. Josiah Wedgwood, M.P., states the case with a *naiveté* which is perfectly refreshing, and wonders how long the door will remain shut in the face of " civilisation." We wish the reader with an unbiassed mind to keep this fact steadily in view, while we proceed with other still more serious considerations. The article before us proceeds with the same frankness :—

"There are two principal methods by which natives are deprived of their free lands and forced to work for wages. The older method, and the one still employed so successfully on the Gold Coast, and, with some modifications, in Sierra Leone, is to assume that a native Chief is already in the same economic position as an English squire, possessing a right to charge rent and to lease or alienate land. This conception of a native is, of course, a European gloss based on the civilisation known to the European. There is no individual in Northern Nigeria who can say, according to native law and custom, this piece of land belongs to me. So said, in 1907, Mr. Temple, now Acting Governor of Northern Nigeria, and no one who has studied the question can doubt that what he said applied, and still applies, to by far the greater part of our Crown Colonies." This form of generalisation, it must be distinctly pointed out, is somewhat dangerous. In any case, we challenge the statement in so far as the Gold Coast is concerned, and we make bold also to state that when examined, even with respect to other parts of West Africa, it will be found that it can only be true in so far as by conquest, cession, or purchase the lands have passed into the hands of the former protecting Power.

And now come the paragraphs upon which attention must be concentrated :—" By far the most usual modern method of depriving natives of their lands," says Mr. Wedgwood, " and of solving the labour

' difficulty,' is the nationalisation and sale method, which we owe to the most ordered and bureaucratic mind of the German and Belgian colonial administration.   This method works as follows : The uncultivated, or, at the least, the unoccupied lands of all our newer Crown Colonies are assumed to be Crown lands, or lands held for the benefit of the public—in some of the public's manifestations.   So it is, in varying degrees and forms, in the Federated Malay States and Seychelles, in Uganda and Nigeria, in Trinidad, British Guiana and Honduras, in Burmah and British East Africa, probably even in the Soudan.   The land is held, as it were, in trust; but the object of the trust and the manner in which the trust is exercised, differs by all the degrees that separate the two Poles, from the working hell of the Congo to the idle paradise of Northern Nigeria.   May I say, in parenthesis, that far more wealth is produced in the Congo ' Free ' State than in Northern Nigeria; the people there work very hard indeed, and if you want people to work hard and produce a great deal of wealth, the Congo system is the best yet invented.''   This is decidedly ominous, and a bit compromising when considered in the light of Mr. Morel's relation to Congo affairs.   Is it possible that, in varying forms, the root idea at the back of even a man like '' E. D. M.'' and his friends is the production of wealth by depriving the natives of free land?   We know that what '' E. D. M.'' writes in the *African Mail* is one thing, and what Mr. Wedgwood writes in the *Aborigines' Bulletin* is another; but Mr. Morel has named Mr. Wedgwood his man, and he cannot blow hot and cold. We have elsewhere shown also that the effect of the Forest Bill, as originally conceived, and before the arguments of counsel whittled it down, was to deprive the natives of free land.   Hence the danger of the situation.   It is difficult in this matter to know who are the real friends of the Natives, who, if even devoid of common intelligence, it is seriously suggested should not even allow their common instinct to point to them wherein their safety lies. It will occur to the reader that, these things being so, " A three-fold danger would seem for the moment to threaten the people of the Gold Coast in the enjoyment of their immemorial rights to their lands. There is the speculator fresh from the Gold-fields of South Africa, who, used to a different system of land tenure, and impatient of the long established rights of the people, based upon their recognised laws and customs, is eager to see such rights swept away with a stroke of the pen, and urges the Government to declare Gold Coast lands Crown lands. There is also the philanthropist who, posing as the heaven-born guardian of native interests, would restrict the people from directly and freely dealing with their lands by placing all business negotiations under Government control and management. There is, again, the native landowner, who, it is alleged, has given cause for Government interference by recklessly dealing with interests in his lands. Between these diverging sentiments, it is possible the ultimate result to the proprietary rights of the aboriginals may be overlooked, and trouble unintentionally caused."

But, to return to the attitude of Mr. Morel and his friends over this land question, as evidenced by Mr. Wedgwood's contribution to the *Bulletin*, it is necessary to emphasise the root evil in the fallacy which has been successfully pointed out in the criticism of the Forest Bill that, as far as the Gold Coast is concerned, there are no Crown lands, the land question on the Gold Coast having been settled as far back as the year 1898. And it must also be pointed out that the history of the West Indian Islands, of British Guiana, of Trinidad, or of the Malay States is not the same as the history of the Gold Coast. There the

Power which has acquired by conquest, cession, or purchase may, or may not, declare a trust in favour of the people.   Here it cannot be so, from the circumstances of the case. You cannot, for the sake of a so-called uniformity, break solemn pledges, and wrench from the hands of those who have trusted you that which is indisputably theirs. But, then, we have internal evidence of what is intended—the avowed purpose of those who hold themselves out as the protectors of the best interests of native rights—those in whose hands the Colonial Office, local officials, and even Parliament, in certain circumstances, may become mere tools.   In the past we have been taught to believe that the noble traditions of the British nation, which governed its conduct in dealing with weak peoples, still control the public conscience. And it is because we fervently cling to such belief that we are persuaded that British public opinion will not tolerate any plans that might be formed by the so-called friends of the indigenes " to prevent the possibility of a landlord class, black or white, ever arising in a Crown Colony."

2

An outstanding feature of the series of articles we have been considering is the importance which the Editor of the *African Mail* attaches to Mr. H. N. Thompson's report on Gold Coast forestry. Before that report was issued, Mr. Thompson had foreshadowed, in an address on " Forestry " to the African Section of the Liverpool Chamber of Commerce, on September 19th, 1904, that soon a Forestry Department would be organised for West Africa. It may, therefore, be safely taken that the report on Gold Coast forestry was the outcome of the policy thus foreshadowed. For this reason, it will be interesting to draw particular attention to an illustrated article specially written for the *West African Mail* by Mr. G. D. Hazzledine, commenting on Mr. H. N. Thompson's address, and which appeared in the October 14th, 1904, issue of that journal. The article in question bore this heading :—

" West African Forests.

" Are they to belong to the Government Official or the Enterprising Merchants?

" Are they to be Preserved or Used?

" A Vital Question for the Trade."

It is necessary to explain that Mr. H. N. Thompson had, on the 19th of September, 1904, as the Conservator of the Forestry and Botanical Departments of Southern Nigeria, delivered an address on Forestry to the African Section of the Liverpool Chamber of Commerce. Mr. Hazzledine, who evidently was present when the address was delivered, had made elaborate notes, and, as it turned out, those notes were made use of in the special article that was contributed to the then *West African Mail*. It is fair, therefore, to suppose that this special contribution had been arranged for by Mr. Morel, and that he was in accord and in sympathy with the views of his special correspondent. The article in question occupies six pages of the paper, and is graphically illustrated throughout. In a masterly summary, Mr. Hazzledine reports Mr. Thompson to have laid down the duties of the Forestry Department as follows :—

(1) " To protect native interests.

(2) " To preserve lasting timber.

(3) " To produce new timber; "

and the use of forestry is represented to be, " because :—

(1) " Ever-green growth is the best check to bush fires, which would denude the country of timber;

(2) " So would unrestricted felling; "
and in dealing with the " methods and objects " of
the Forestry Department, to " get data for preparation of the best *working plan* " is, *inter alia*, referred
to.

To judge from the storm of apparent indignation
with which the address was received by the Chamber,
it is not surprising that Mr. Hazzledine, as the spokes-
man in the Press of the Chamber, spared no pains in
showing up the main fallacies in Mr. Thompson's
arguments. Said he, in his report, " it was evident,
from the short but pointed discussion which the
address immediately provoked from leading members
of the Chamber who had listened to it, that the first
part was quite objectionable," such first part " dealing with mahogany and other timber."

I am but introducing the position of the *West
African Mail's* special correspondent in 1904 to the
intelligent public, and, so, I will let Mr. Hazzledine
take up the argument in his own way. It appears
that Mr. Thompson had suggested certain forest
regulations, which he had accidentally called the
" usual regulations," forgetting that what is "usual"
is not *always* what is practicable, desirable, or expedient. Let us see what these " usual regulations "
were. They were stated thus :—

(1) " Allow some areas to be exploited, and
preserve others intact

(2) " Limit the number of trees to be felled each
year.

(3) " Forbid the felling of trees not yet mature,
or within a fixed age of maturity, *e.g.*, in
the case of mahogany, fixing a minimum
growth; "

and in dealing with the " Procedure of the Department," " Preparation of *working plan* and super-

vision and inspection to enforce *working plan* '' are
prominently referred to.

After fairly and fully epitomising the address. Mr.
Hazzledine had no hesitation in insisting that the regulations imposed by the Southern Nigerian Forestry
and Botanical Department must be withdrawn. Said
he :—'' The above is full and fair epitome of the
address; no attempt has been made to suppress any
of the words or pervert any of the arguments, for it
is wished to meet them as they are, and deal with
them in the same spirit as that in which they are propounded. No advantage would be gained by being
unfair with them; they are not merely the arguments
of the lecturer, they are the arguments of the Department, the arguments of the Government, the arguments which have been listened to, and which have
produced the recent timber regulations which are
so objectionable to the merchants engaged in the
West African timber trade. There is no doubt, in
their minds, that the regulations ought to be withdrawn, that they were hastily propounded, were only
half thought out, and were carelessly worded. They
must be withdrawn, or the trade will be killed.''

Now, in all that we have written upon the Forest
Bill of 1911, we have said nothing quite so strong as
this. If this is so, considering that in the Forest Bill,
1911, upon the constitution of forest reserves man-
ageable by Government not even the owner can
then grant a concession or collect produce from his
own land, or use it in any way, without the Governor's
consent, it becomes important and relevant to ask
whether this is a policy which commends itself to
practical statesmanship.

For years past a good trade in forest produce in
the Gold Coast has been induced, but dependent abso-

lutely upon the energetic co-operation of the indigenes.
Will matters be improved by practically declaring
their lands Crown lands, by restricting and imposing
burdens upon their use thereof, by filling them with
vague suspicions, by creating an agrarian grievance
of the first magnitude?

But we must patiently follow the special correspondent while he exposes the weak points in the Government forestry scheme.   The first good point he makes
is that Mr. Thompson, like most Indian Service men,
had made the palpable mistake of applying Indian
conditions to West African conditions, which are not
the same.   He makes it clear that what Mr. Thompson lays down as to the danger of denudation, the
perils of the encroaching desert and desert fires, &c.,
while sound in Upper Burmah, "may be quite
wrongly applied to the conditions prevailing in the
dense tropical West African forest belt, which is
gifted with the proverbial thousand and one differences, mostly unascertained."   Continuing, he says :
"It is believed that there is more mature timber in
the belt than man can reasonably expect to exhaust,
and, if so, the evil of such impossible exhaustion need
not enter the premises."   To clear our minds of any
possible difference in the forests of the Gold Coast and
Nigeria, it may be stated that Mr. Thompson was
selected, after dealing with Nigerian forestry, to prepare a report on the forestry of the Gold Coast, and
from the subsequent reports of the Conservator for
the Gold Coast, based to a large extent upon Mr.
Thompson's premises, it is almost certain that
Nigerian physical conditions are practically the same
as those of the Gold Coast.   It will, therefore, be
useful here to quote the Gold Coast Conservator of
Forests as to the inexhaustibleness, for all practical
purposes, of the timber areas of the Gold Coast.   In
his report of June 16th, 1911, published in the

Government Gazette of December 2nd, 1911, he
says :—

" As a description of the forests passed through
day by day during this tour would entail constant
repetition, it is only necessary to say that the whole
of the country is extremely well wooded with a great
wealth of excellent timber, with patches here and
there of forest rich in rubber trees and vines. The
latter have been exploited to the fullest extent, but
the timber generally has not been utilised, except in
the vicinity of rivers, where mahoganies have usually
been selected for canoes."

Our special correspondent next proceeds to knock
the bottom out of the oft-repeated argument of keeping up " the *normal forest capital*, as represented by a
forest which has a possibility of a certain regular
number of mature trunks a year." Exposing the
fallacy, he says :—" The theory sounds excellent,
but it is quite possible that such normality would be
wasteful. To make us admit that it would be the
most desirable condition, it is also necessary to postu-
late a regular demand. Now, that regular yearly
demand is exactly what never prevails. The demand,
for example, for African mahogany is not regular
year by year ; a thousand things may cause it to fluc-
tuate, fashion amongst others, and the exploiter who
reserved his trunks, relying on one year's demand
being repeated, might be landed without a market
when he got them down to the coast—without a
market, that is, which would make it profitable to
ship them home." Other circumstances may occur
to the reader making it wholly undesirable to lay
down fast rules as to the reservation of timber areas.
All this seems to have struck " E. D. M." forcibly
in 1904. But he may be inclined to controvert the
arguments of his special correspondent in 1913.

A serious flaw in the official syllogism is pointed out

in these words :—" From the premises ' the world's
timber is in danger of being exhausted,' the conclusion, therefore, it is advisable to restrict the output
of coast timber, cannot be admitted.   To put it
another way, three-quarters of the world's timber
might be ablaze, and yet the Coast trunks might be
the same temperature as they have been for the last
200 years, and quite out of danger of sparks." And
when we remember that it takes about 200 years for
a mahogany tree to mature, it is reasonable to consider that the need of afforestation need not enter the
purview of practical constructive statesmanship.
According to our correspondent, it is not the duty of
Government to look so far ahead.   " No human
foresight is strong enough to pierce the veil of years
like that."   What actually does happen on the Gold
Coast at least, is this : A band of natives club themselves together and cut timber along the creeks and
float them down the rivers to the coast on the tribute
system.   That is the main way in which the trade is
replenished and kept up.   This system pre-supposes
free access to the ancestral lands, of which both
Chief and people are joint-owners.   Will shutting
the door practically in the face of the native cutter,
by the enforcement of the provisions of the Forest
Bill, improve matters?

A significant illustration may be found on page 678
of the particular issue of the *West African Mail* we
are discussing, above the title, " A little clearing
would be useful here."   And a striking picture of
dense vegetation it is, which is a common characteristic feature of the West African forests.   The illustration is to point the moral that, however sound the
theory that forests should be allowed to stand " because they shelter the soil from wind and atmospheric
agencies, and preserve the productiveness of the
soil," may be, such a theory does not necessarily

apply to West Africa; and the argument is clinched
by a quotation from Mr. Thompson's own report,
where he says:—'' In the ever-green forests, however, these light and buoyant (rubber) seeds experience some difficulty in reaching the soil, owing to
the dense-leafed canopy and other growth existing
in such localities.   It is, therefore, necessary, in
order to stimulate the natural regeneration of the
species, that advantage should be taken of the tem-
porary clearing made by the natives for their farms.''
As to this, the special correspondent remarks:—
'' Could anything more clearly show that the argument of fear of denudation has no bottom in it?
Even if shelter were required, whether to break
winds or for any other purpose, it is possible that all
the marketable trunks which can be got at could be
removed without spoiling shelter.   There are, unfortunately, too many trees not worth felling.''   As far
as the Gold Coast is concerned, it is worth pressing
home the view of the Forest Conservator that the
timber areas have scarcely been touched, and that
for best of all reasons that, except along the banks
of the rivers and railway, it is not generally worth
the trouble, nor would it pay to cut them.   In a few
well-chosen sentences, Mr. Hazzledine disposes of
the fallacy that it is the duty of the Government to
preserve existing timber.   '' The second duty,'' says
he, '' is utterly bad . . . it is the preservation of
existing timber. . . .   The duty of Government in
Southern Nigeria, as regards existing timber, is to
assist the natives and the traders by every possible
manner of means in converting into national wealth
whatever timber exists.   For the natives it means
civilisation, for the traders prosperity, and, as a
consequence of both, it means revenue to the Government.''   But it will be seen that the idea of the
Government coming in as a kind of middleman between the traders and the natives, according to our

correspondent, may not be a blessing. It is suggested that by encouraging and fostering legitimate business between the native and the trader, and not insisting upon artificial preservation, all concerned would benefit, including the Government. From this point of view, it becomes easy to follow our special correspondent when he suggests what the proper duties of a Forestry Department should rather be, in these words :—

(1) " To see justice done between natives and traders.

(2) " To assist both in the conversion of existing timber into wealth.

(3) " To plant and cultivate these forest products which will, with reasonable certainty and in reasonable time, prove remunerative."

It is not necessary to follow our special correspondent much longer, beyond observing that he draws particular attention to the fact that " in the transport difficulty, there is a check to denudation." Yes, when the Government will have provided the Gold Coast with good roads and canals, subsidiary lines of railway to connect trunk lines, and in other ways overcome the practical question of transport, so as to make it possible for cutters to exploit the timber areas yet untouched, it may be time enough then, if necessary, to consider the passing of laws for the preservation of Gold Coast timber. " To prevent timber being converted into wealth," winds up our special correspondent, " *lest* perchance it should turn out to have been better to have let it stand a little longer, while there is quite an equal probability that subsequent exploration will reveal better timber, and spoil the market for that now discovered altogether; to restrict the freedom of trade on hypothesis, and without *knowing* whether it is right or wrong to do so, is not good government—it is not common sense. It only leads to disaster, and of the folly of it no more glaring instance can be imagined than the root rubber regulations, of which Mr. Thompson himself says :—' The old regulations applying to the extraction of root rubber, under the supposition that such rubber was collected from the roots of the *Funtumia* and species of the *Landolphia* not possessing *rhizomes*, now that it is known that it is only extracted from species possessing rhizomes, require alteration.' Require alteration, forsooth! And what about the natives who have been taught that it is a crime to collect root rubber—how are they to be untaught? How, too, is the trade which might have been done to be done now? How are the profits which might have been made to be made now? How are the years which might have passed to be recalled?'' Perhaps Mr. Morel will refuse to admit the force of these significant considerations now.

CHAPTER V.

THE LEGAL ASPECTS OF THE MATTER.

The principles of Gold Coast land tenure are well ascertained and admit of no ambiguity. In the two pamphlets, which were published on behalf of the Kings and Chiefs of the Central and Western Provinces of the Gold Coast in conference with the Gold Coast Aborigines Rights Protection Society, I dealt fully with the historical part of the subject. I propose now to deal with the principles appertaining thereto.

There is no conception which is clearer to the mind of a student of Gold Coast Customary Law than the broad distinction between paramountcy and ownership. And this may be traced in all the standard works on the subject. Happily for the present writer this distinction has been indicated by him in " Gold Coast Native Institutions." So that the summary that is here given is devoid of controversy.

From time immemorial lands in this country have been held by family groups, the members of each family being such persons as can trace a clear descent from one maternal ancestress. Succession runs through the female line, and a brother by the same mother, or a nephew being the son of one's maternal sister, would succeed to a man's property, and not his son. Failing succession in the female line, a " domestic " would succeed for the reason that the Customary Law regards him as a member of the family.

But such succession does not imply that the successor, as the head of the family for the time being, has vested in him the right of ownership to the exclusion of the other members of the family.   He is, indeed, a co-owner with the rest; and so jealously do the members of the family restrict him to a legitimate use of his position that the slightest trespass on their rights entails deposition.   Theirs is the right to nominate to the headship of the family. Theirs is the right to depose from such headship; and no act of the head for the time being is valid without the consent and concurrence of the members of the family, nor is his permission necessary in the enjoyment of the family land.   At Page 169 of Sarbah's '' Fanti Law Reports '' the case of Mary Barnes v. Chief Quasie Atta is quoted, wherein it is laid down that '' not even the regular occupant could alienate property without some concurrence by the people of the Stool, who have an interest in it, and are usually consulted in such a matter.''

In the same Reports, at Page 170, we read in the case of Quamina Awortchie v. Cudjoe Eshon that, '' If the purchaser knows that the land he had to purchase was a family land and the man from whom he was purchasing it was the head of that family, he would not make the purchase from the head without requesting him to get the concurrence of his family, and if he violated this his money was considered lost, as he was fully aware that the land was family land.''

And it is of the utmost importance to note that this principle applies equally to the head of a family whether he occupies a subordinate or a superior stool.

Thus it will be seen the danger of employing the terminalogy of English Law.   A successor in the English system has sole control and ownership.   In the Customary Law he is a co-owner, and has no such control.

Nor is the successor a trustee in the sense of Equity Jurisprudence. The rights of the Chief in respect of land is not separable from those of his people who have a conjoint right in the property as well as a joint control. A Chief cannot make a grant without such consent and concurrence. A trustee controls the funds of the *cestui qui trust*. A Chief has no such control, but must immediately, upon realisation, share the proceeds with his people. The trustee is owner for the time being, exercising the rights of ownership for the *cestui qui trust*. In the Customary Law this is not so, since the people never at any time divest themselves of their rights and the active exercise thereof in favour of the trustee. In short, the Chief is joint-owner of the property, and he is the head of his people, who share every interest in the property with him. Hence it is important to note that the English Law of Trusts does not apply to Gold Coast Land Tenure. And the term " trustee " where it occurs in this summary must be taken with that qualification.

Now what are the rights of the King in respect of the lands of a community? The King, *qua* king, does not own all the lands of the State. The limits of his proprietary rights are strictly defined.

There are, first of all, lands which are the ancestral property of the King. These he can deal with as he pleases, but with the sanction of the members of his family.

Secondly, there are lands attached to the stool which the King can deal with only with the consent of the Councillors.†

Thirdly, there are the general lands of the State over which the King exercises paramountcy. It is a

---

† The African (West) Exploitation and Development Syndicate Ltd., v. Sir Alfred Kirby and the Princes River Gold Mines, Ltd.

sort of sovereign oversight which does not carry with
it the ownership of any particular land. It is not
even ownership in a general way in respect of which,
per se, the King can have a *locus standi* in a court of
law. To him, indeed, belongs the power of ratifying
and confirming what the subject grants, though he
may not himself grant that which is given. Such
ratification is not even absolutely essential to make
the transaction valid, though as being evidence of
good faith, such ratification or confirmation is re-
sorted to and is, indeed, becoming quite common in
modern grants. Nor is it difficult to see the reason of
this. In the early stages of the Native State System,
upon the acquisition of lands by conquest or settle-
ment by members of a given community, the lands
so acquired or settled upon would be apportioned
among those worthy of them in the order of merit.
Upon that basis, the Chief Military Commander, who
subsequently becomes the King, would have his
requisite share, and so would every member of the
community down to the lowest ranks of the fighting
men. Thus, each man's land would be his own special
property and that of his family, though the King, as
overlord of all, would, undoubtedly, exercise
sovereignty over the whole land, every inch of which,
however, would have an individual family owning it.

Bearing in mind the foregoing preliminary observations, we may now proceed to discuss the fundamental
principles of Paramountcy.

At the outset we must rid our minds of misconcep-
tions. And here we must carefully distinguish
between Paramountcy and Ownership. But is Ownership in the Customary Law the same as Ownership in
Roman Law? If we examine the incidents thereof in
the two systems, we shall find that there is an important difference.

In the time of Justinian, at all events, Roman

society had advanced beyond the communistic stage. It was possible even then to speak of the owner's right to possess as a right against all the world, a right *in rem*. Indeed, so far had the notion of exclusive possession gone, that a person, *sui juris*, could pass his property by will. In the early stage of testamentary disposition, it is true, the appointment of an heir to continue the legal personality of the testator was the primary idea; but later, we come to find the Roman will making the heir a mere trustee for the distribution of property.

But in the Customary Law, we find no trace of individual ownership. What the head of a family acquires to-day in his own individual right will, in the next generation, be quite indistinguishable from the general ancestral property of which he was a trustee. Even during his lifetime the person on the stool scarcely makes a difference in his own mind between what he received as family property and what he adds thereto by his exertions. And the law of succession furnishes the best reason for the phenomenon. Both what came to the head of the family and what he has made pass, at his death, to his uterine brother, cousin, or nephew, as the case may be, who being the only possible and legitimate successor to the stool-holder, the latter gladly regards as the trustee in one sense, and one of the beneficiaries in another sense, of all after his death.

With this important qualification, namely, that the family in the Customary Law is the unit for the purpose of ownership, we may now proceed to distinguish Ownership from Paramountcy.

The notion is somewhat common that where a Chief pays tribute to another, the latter is necessarily the paramount Chief of the former. But this is only a loose way of applying the term "paramount." Tribute is not only payable to a Chief, but to any person holding land in the country say, as head of a family, by whose leave another person works upon the family lands. It would be absurd to call the licensor in such a case the paramount Chief of the licensee. Take an extreme case, and the absurdity will appear all the clearer. A has a portion of the family lands alloted her for the purpose of growing ground nuts thereon. A allows B, her friend, to till a portion of the ground on the understanding that B will give her one-third share of the in-gathering crop. In what possible sense is A " paramount " to B?

It is clear, therefore, that the payment of *abusa*, one-third share, is not the test of Paramountcy; it merely indicates the person having the right *to possess*. Indeed, the custom of the paramount Chief to receive an occasional contribution, be it small or be it large, is in respect of allegiance due to him by a subordinate Chief. Where a paramount Chief happens to receive *abusa*, that is, one-third share, of the proceeds of land, then it is by reason of the fact that the right *to possess* is ultimately traceable to his stool. Thus, we have the case where a person receives a portion, usually a third, *abusa*, of the proceeds of a sale of land by a licensee of that person; and the case where a paramount Chief receives a customary present, the extent of it depending upon circumstances, upon the happening of any event in respect of which the subordinate may suitably mark his allegiance to the superior Chief. The latter may be called the custom of *occasional contribution* to the superior Chief; the former, the right of the owner, or the person having the right to possess, to *abusa*, one-third share. Much confusion of ideas would be saved by confining the term " *tribute* " to the case where a licensee is under obligation to make one-third payment to a licensor, and " *allegiance fee* " to the case where a vassal is expected to acknowledge the sovereignty of a paramount Chief by the customary present.

In Ashanti, where a stranger kills big game on another's land, the licensee takes to the licensor a portion of the meat, the latter, in turn, taking to the Head Chief a leg of the animal killed. Again, where a nugget is found in mining, the licensee brings to the licensor a portion of the gold with the nugget, the licensor sending the nugget to the King. In the two cases, the licensor would be the person having the right *to possess*, the Head Chief or King merely having a claim to the *allegiance* of the licensor. Hence the importance of using " tribute " to denote what is contributed to the licensor, and the phrase " allegiance fee" to what the licensee offers to the overlord. *Tribute* would thus be an incident of Ownership, while *allegiance* would be an incident of Paramountcy.

In the *Impatassi* case† expert evidence was given by Atta, King of Axim. The question was asked : " Was tribute ever instituted in respect of the sovereignty of one stool over the other?"

Answer : " The person on whose land you have settled, although his stool may be small, can claim tribute. Tribute is paid in respect of ownership."

In giving judgment, the learned judge remarked :

" Now, from the evidence of the King of Axim, it appears that the right to demand and receive tribute on land is based on ownership, and I am of opinion that on Ownership also must be based the right to give or withhold consent to dealings with land. It may possibly be that by custom in some cases a Chief can claim tribute from his sub-Chiefs in

---

† Opposed Enquiries, Nos. 164 and 169, Axim. *Coram* Morgan, J. ; Renner and Williams for Defendants, Hayford for Grantors, Ribeiro for Opposer : Axim Records, February, 1902.

respect of their lands apart from the question of ownership of such land, but in such cases I do not think that his consent would be necessary to render valid dealings with land the right to hold and occupy which was not derived from his family or town stool."

This case went up to the Court of Appeal which sat at Cape Coast in October, 1902,† which affirmed the judgment of the Court below, declaring the concessions, the subject of the enquiries, to be invalid on the ground that the consent of the opposer had neither been asked for nor obtained, the right of the grantors of the concessions, the subject of the enquiries, to hold and occupy the lands comprised therein being derived through and from the stool on which the opposer was now sitting, and that the opposer's consent was necessary for the valid leasing of the said lands.

On the 6th of October, 1902, counsel for the claimants moved *ex parte* " for leave to appeal from the judgment of the Full Court, dated 1st October, 1902, refusing to grant special leave to appeal from the judgment of the Divisional Court of 28th April, 1902, at Axim," and the Full Court, in ruling upon the motion, took opportunity to emphasise the point that in its opinion the judgment of the Court below " is right," and " is supported by the evidence."

The Full Court, therefore, clearly supported the proposition that " the right to demand and receive tribute on land is based on ownership . . . and that on ownership also must be based the right to give or withhold consent to dealings with land."

Having shown that tribute pure and simple is really an incident of Ownership in the Customary Law, and

† *Coram* Sir Brandford Griffith, C.J. ; Smith, J. and Nicoll, J. ; Hayford for Grantors, Renner and Williams for Claimants, Savage for Opposer : Cape Coast Appeal Records, October, 1902.

that the obligation of a vassal to render allegiance fee
to his superior lord is erroneously termed tribute, it
will be interesting now to discuss "allegiance," the
bond which unites the superior Chief, usually a King,
to his vassal.

Allegiance, then, is that personal relationship
between the occupants of two stools whereby the inferior acknowledges the authority of the superior
over him.   Such acknowledgment may take the form
of military or other service, and occasionally an allegiance fee.   Such relationship has nothing to do with
the lands of the vassal.   It may happen that the
superior lord is at the same time the licensor of the
vassal in respect of his holding, but that will be
merely accidental.

That allegiance is personal and not territorial is
seen from a number of instances in the history of certain communities of the country.   Take, for example,
the case of the Akataki people, known as the
Commendas.   Now, it is an historical fact that the
people of Akataki originally came from Akatakiwa in
the Inkusukum district, the present head being the
well-known King Essandor.   Now, if you trace the
etymology of the two words Akataki and Akatakiwa,
you will find that the one is the feminine form of
the other.   Whether it be that Akataki, the masculine
form of the word, was chosen by the people of Commenda to indicate their origin, or whether Akataki,
the brother of Akatakiwa, founded the present town
of Commenda matters little; but there can be no doubt
about it that the two branches of the Inkusukum
people have always recognised the same origin, the
Akataki people owing allegiance to the paramount
King, Essandor.   Such relation is personal, and has
no territorial significance; but it is, nevertheless, as
vital in the conceptions of Native Institutions as Succession is to property in the Customary Law.

The case of Apenquah† is in point. It came before His Excellency Governor E. B. Andrews in Council at Cape Coast, on the 7th of February, 1861. The main point in the case was whether or not Apenquah, being a subject of the stool of King Chibbo of Assin, could rid himself of his allegiance to the stool or transfer his allegiance to another stool. Said the Court : " It has been decided long since that Apenquah was not a private slave to any person, but that he was a subject of the stool of Assin Chibbo, and at this day is consequently a subject of Amba Danquah, Regent of Southern Assin, and, according to strict law, he cannot rid himself of the allegiance to the stool.

" The Court has taken into its serious consideration the importance of this case. There are grave questions involved; the most important, and that which in this peculiar country might be practised with the most serious consequences to the well-being and tranquility of the Protectorate, is a proceeding similar to that which the Court is now called upon to decide as to its legality, it being whether a man occupying a considerable position, as does Apenquah, can suddenly march off with a number of his Prince's lawful subjects, and deliver himself and them to a rival Chief.

" The Court is of opinion that Apenquah does not possess the right to leave his sovereign Amba Danquah, with all his people, and place himself under Inkee, and that he has not been able to show any grounds on which he could complain of bad treatment towards him by his sovereign. . . .

" For the future, it is to be distinctly laid down that a headman, captain, or Chief shall not be suffered

† See Sarbah's "Fanti Customary Laws," p. 203 ; also, idem, the case of Quamin Dansue v. Tchibu-Darcoon and Cancan, p. 130.

to transfer his allegiance with his followers to the Chief or Prince of another country. Neither shall he be allowed to domicile in another country as a captain with his followers, though he may not have removed his allegiance to his former Prince.

" To act thus shall be held to be treason, the punishment being the loss of all property and degradation of rank within the Protectorate, such headman, captain, or chief to be given up with his followers, it being a high crime, the Prince harbouring them to be deposed from his stool. But where a headman, captain, or chief is of full age, and wishes to domicile in another country, and is a free man, he shall be permitted to do so, taking with him his one wife and children by that wife; at the same time he shall not transfer his allegiance to the Prince of his adopted country as a captain, but retire to live under that Prince as a private man, leaving all his possessions, which become forfeited to the sovereign whose country he has quitted."

Our early Administrators and the Judicial Assessors somehow always managed to get to the core of Native Institutions. It may be because they took the precaution not to decide a given point without collecting the opinions of native Councillors, competent to advise upon the point in issue. Thus, it happens that Apenquah's case states the doctrines of allegiance in a form intelligible and scientific.

We gather the essential features of Allegiance, then, to be :—

1. That it is a personal relationship which has nothing to do with property rights.

2. That a subject holding any public position in a country cannot transfer his allegiance at will without forfeiting his rank and " all his possessions to the sovereign whose country he has quitted."

And the doctrines of Allegiance have the sanction of sound common sense.

But what happens where the subjects of a native King found a colony in another district with the sanction of such King, as in the case of the Akatakiwa colonists settling at Akataki, Commenda? It would follow, as a matter of course, that they would carry with them the protection of their King, and, consequently, they would remain loyal to him and owe him allegiance. Here they would pay tribute for the land they have settled upon to the owner of that land; while they would repair occasionally to their ancient and mother country with suitable presents to the paramount King, and which we have called "allegiance fee." If the paramount King went to war, he would call for the services of his children over sea or over country. Hence you have the phenomenon in a given war of seeing the people of even a small town dividing themselves under the banners of contesting paramount Kings.

When the reason of things begins to dawn upon one, one is moved to pity the helplessness of present-day Administrators of the country, who are in the dark as to why, for example, Essandor, King of all the Inkusukums, should tenaciously cling to the tie of allegiance which unites Akataki with Akatakiwa; or why people in the far west end of the country should wish to preserve their allegiance to one paramount King instead of to another.

We may now usefully and satisfactorily address ourselves to the question, whether the paramount King's consent is necessary to the validity of a grant of land? If you confine the term "paramount" to its legitimate and appropriate use in the way I have above explained, we can answer the question only in the negative.

In the Esubankassa and Indumsuasu Opposed Enquiries,* which raised the important issue of Paramountcy, expert evidence as to consent was given. The Court examined Quamina Annobil, the principal linguist of the King of Lower Wassaw.   Said he: "The under Chief can sell land without the head Chief's consent; he only gives him a share of the money." This evidence, coming from the linguist of the King of Lower Wassaw, where almost every Chief pays tribute to the King, or, in substitution thereof, has handed to the King a portion of his lands, is remarkable.   But it denotes clearly the general rule of which the particular tenure of lands in the Wassaw country is, perhaps, the sole exception.

The Court, in its judgment, found "that the King of Beyin is not the owner of any of these lands. The owners of these lands must, however, report to the King *before* they dispose thereof." The italics are mine.   This case also went up to the Court of Appeal,† which sat at Cape Coast on the 6th October, 1902, the same Court which decided the Impatassi case; and the judgment of the Court below was upheld.   Let us now recall the express words of the judgment of the Court below in the Impatassi case. They are: "I am of opinion that on ownership also must be based the right to give or withhold consent to dealings with land," from which proposition the Full Court did not dissent.   Clearly, the two judgments are in conflict with one another.   Assuming that the owner of land only has the right to give or withhold consent, why must a person who is not such owner be informed before the owner of the land dis-

* Opposed Enquiries, Nos. 150 and 343. *Coram* Nicoll J. ; Williams for Aka Ayima, Hayford for Yamike Kwekuu and Blay ; Ribeiro and Addo for Vanderpuye : Axim Records, June, 1902.

† Opposed Enquiries, Nos. 150 and 343. *Coram* Sir Brandford Griffith, C.J., Smith, J., and Nicoll, J. ; Hayford for Appellants, Yamike Kweku and Blay ; Renner and Williams for Respondent, Aka Ayima : Cape Coast Appeal Records, October, 1902.

poses thereof? One can only come to the conclusion that the Full Court failed to draw the distinction between " tribute," payable to a landowner, and a customary present, " allegiance fee," rendered to a paramount Chief after the owner, it may be, has disposed of his land, and not necessarily in respect of such disposal. The point is an important one, and it is to be hoped that some day the Appeal Court will patiently hear it argued out, and the full weight of its learning and authority brought to bear upon a vital point in Native Institutions.

The learned author of " Fanti Customary Laws " has remarked upon this matter thus :—

" Where the concession is made by a subordinate Chief, enquiries should be made to find out whether the concurrence of his paramount Chief is necessary or no, for whatever lawful grant or permission is so given by a person *de facto* Chief with the concurrence of men *de facto* members of the village council or stool, is good and valid according to Customary Law, and the grantee by taking possession of the land and working thereon becomes a tenant of the stool, village council, or family, as the case may be, and not of a specific individual."†

Here we find one of the best authorities on the subject making it clear that the " concurrence " of the paramount Chief may or may not be necessary.

As I have before shown, the only possible case in which the paramount Chief's " concurrence " or " consent " will be necessary is where such paramount Chief's stool is the root of the licensee's title, while, at the same time, the licensee owes allegiance to the stool of the licensor. If care is taken, as suggested, to use the terms " tribute " and " allegiance fee " in their proper connections, there need be no confusion of ideas.

---

† P. 57.

Ownership, then, must be carefully distinguished from Paramountcy. The principles involved in the foregoing discussion may be embodied in a few simple rules :—

1. A gives permission to B to settle on Daman Land. The permissee becomes a tenant at will, who, so long as he does not claim adversely to the permissor, will be supported by the permissor in his holding. But the moment the permissee sets up adverse title to the land, the permissor's ownership or right *to possess* revives as against the permissee's right *of possession*.

2. While the permission subsists, the permissee would be liable to contribute one-third, *abusa*, of the proceeds of the land to the permissor, whose consent would be absolutely necessary before the permissee could validly deal with the land.

3. A is B's paramount King. B holds lands, title to which is not derived from A's stool. A has only a right to B's allegiance; and the customary present (which I have called " allegiance fee ") which B brings to A from time to time is certainly not tribute in the sense that A can exact it as of right. Such personal relation between A and B is Paramountcy pure and simple, which has nothing to do with property rights.

4. The paramount King, as such, has no right to exact tribute, nor is his consent necessary to make a grant valid.

5. Tribute is an incident of Ownership, in other words, of the relationship subsisting between landlord and tenant.

6. Allegiance is an incident of Paramountcy, indicated sometimes by the rendering of " allegiance fee."

7. Indeed, it does happen that a superior Chief holds lands of an inferior Chief, and a Chief of a commoner.

From the foregoing it is abundantly clear that the paramount Chief of a Native State is in no sense the *ultimus haeres* to any land to which there is no succession, since in the Customary Law care is taken to continue the *persona* of the family. Where blood relatives in the maternal line and " domestics " fail, a tribesman, by adoption and commendation, will be called in to continue the *persona* of the family.

It is also clear, of course, that the British Crown can possess no inherent right of *ultimus haeres* to any land for which no other owner can be found. Happily, this matter has received the attention of so distinguished a writer as Mr. A. W. Hayes Redwar, Barrister-at-Law, who for many years was a Puisne Judge of the Supreme Court of the Gold Coast, in his " Comments on some Ordinances of the Gold Coast Colony, with a few decided cases." The learned author, writing on " Tenure and Inheritance," says, at Page 68 :—

" It is important, in the first place, to notice that in
" accordance with the policy of the British Government,
" which followed that of the London Committee of
" African Merchants administering the affairs of the
" Settlements on the Gold Coast (see Dispatch dated
" October 20th, 1836, addressed by the Committee in
" London to their Chief Magistrate at Cape Coast Castle,
" published in Sarbah's ' Fanti Constitution,' at p. 223),
" the Crown lays claim to no territorial possession over
" any portion of the Gold Coast, and that, except as
" regards the actual site of the Forts and Castles and any
" lands specially acquired by purchase for public purposes
" under the Public Lands Ordinance, 1876, the Crown
" does not own the soil of the Colony. Legislative recog-
" nition of this position of affairs, and especially as
" regards the native ownership of the land, is given
" directly or indirectly by the provisions of various local

" Ordinances. By the Public Lands Ordinance, 1876,
" provision is made for the acquisition by compulsory
" purchase by the Colonial Secretary in trust for the
" Sovereign of such lands as may be required for the ser-
" vice of the Colony, upon payment of compensation to
" the owners thereof, or parties having any interest in
" such lands. By the Marriage Ordinance, 1884, s. 39,
" it is enacted that where by the law any portion of the
" real or personal estate, other than native family pro-
" perty, of persons married under its provisions, and
" dying intestate and without next of kin, would become a
" portion of the hereditary revenue of the Crown (*i.e.*,
" by ' escheat,' or as bona vacantia), such portion shall
" be distributed in accordance with the Native Law of
" Succession, ' and shall not become a portion of the said
" casual hereditary revenue.' It will thus be seen that
" in the only case in which escheat could occur (viz.,
" where natives, by contracting monogamous marriage,
" have changed their status, and brought their Individual
" Property within the rules of English Law under Section
" 14 of the Supreme Court Ordinance) the Legislature
" interferes to prevent escheat. It should be remembered
" that escheat is purely an incident of the possession of
" lands held under tenure from the Crown, which cannot
" exist when the Crown, by its responsible officer and
" through the medium of the Colonial Legislature, has
" disclaimed the right as *ultimus haeres* to the reversion.
" There are, therefore, no lands at the Gold Coast which
" devolve on the Crown on intestacy and failure of heirs,
" and there is no Tenure from the Crown as regards the
" native landowners who are not tenants in fee simple
" (the largest known to English law, which is still liable
" to the incident of ' escheat ' to the Crown by its ultimate
" reversionary right), but absolute owners."

In support of such disclaimer, the learned author
quotes from Hansard, vol. 167, p. 125, 11th December, 1906, the reply in the House of Commons of Mr.
Winston Churchill, the then Under-Secretary of State
for the Colonies, to a question by the late Sir Charles
Dilke, M.P., as follows :—

" In West Africa there is very little land at the disposal
" of Government, but the land generally is in the owner-
" ship of Native Chiefs or Tribes."

That this is so may also be gathered from the history of Native Jurisdiction. In the year 1907 the Colonial Government sought to pass a Native Jurisdiction Ordinance which suggested the conferring of Jurisdiction on the Kings and Chiefs. This was strongly opposed by them, with the result that the "Native Jurisdiction Ordinance, 1911," merely regulates the Jurisdiction inherent in the Native Kings and Chiefs which had, since October 24th, 1887, been affirmed by the judgment of the Appeal Court of the Gold Coast in the case of Oppon v. Ackinnie *Coram* McLeod, C.J., Smallman Smith, J., and Francis Smith, J. In the Judgment of the learned Judges we read : —

" Without discussing whether a Governor has power to " take away inherent jurisdiction, and without pretending " to understand what the Full Court meant by the words " ' unless those powers are taken away by the Governor,' " we cannot help regarding the suggested line of criticism " as unworthy of comment.

" Had it not been for the opinion of Bailey, C.J., we " would have entertained no doubt upon the question " which we have discussed. Now that we have considered " it from every possible point of view, we are clear that " the Supreme Court Ordinance, 1876, has in no way " impaired the judicial powers of native kings and chiefs, " and, so far as we know, it has not been suggested that " any other Ordinance has taken them away."

In September, 1907, the Chief Justice of the Gold Coast in the case of Mutchi v. Kobine Annan, Kobina Inketsia, Mutchi v. Kudo again affirmed the same position laid down in Oppon v. Ackinnie by showing that in nothing that had happened since 1887 had the jurisdiction been impaired, as was evident from the existence of Native Courts and prisons.

Again, it is of considerable importance to note that the words "tribe" and "family" are not synonymous terms in the conception of the Customary Law. We

have already indicated the meaning of the term
"family." The members of a tribe, say the
"Agona," may reside in remote parts. Though the
members thereof are of the same "clan," they are
not of the same blood, nor can they claim, as of right,
to succeed to one another. There are, for example,
"Agona" tribesmen residing in Ashanti who cannot
possibly have any claim to the lands of "Agona"
tribesmen in Fantiland, nor, for that matter, can a
tribesman from a neighbouring village claim, as of
right, succession to the property of a tribesman of
the next village. Descent and succession are through
the blood; failing blood, then come in "domestics";
failing "domestics," then tribesmen only by commendation or adoption. In other words, it would seem
that in the remote past there was some visible tangible
connection between the members of a tribe, but such
connection is lost in tradition; and it is enough to
say that in property considerations one goes hopelessly wrong in the conception of the Customary Law
when he applies the terms "family" and "tribe"
synonymously. For this reason the phrases "tribal
stool" and "tribal lands," as applied to proprietary
rights in the Customary Law, are meaningless.

It is not part of my scheme to discuss the Law of
Tenure as it applies to other parts of West Africa.
But I believe it can be taken as a fundamental proposition applicable to nearly all, that in West Africa
"there can be no land without an owner." It is not
difficult to trace this principle in the Gambia, in
Sierra Leone, or in Southern Nigeria. And some day
a Jurist will arise who will give us a comparative
study of the land systems of the different Dependencies. Then will it be seen that, in whatever way presented, the true view is that the West African is un-
alterably attached to his land, and that, legally, his
status cannot be changed to that of a serf.

CHAPTER VI.

HISTORICAL SUMMARY.

We propose now to present a connected account of the principal events relating to the West African land question from the fall of 1911, when counsel were heard at the Legislative Council of the Gold Coast, down to the time of writing, April, 1913. Of the earlier period of this controversy I have said enough in the two pamphlets to which reference has already been made.

Through the energy of the Gold Coast Aborigines' Rights Protection Society, in conference with the Kings and Chiefs of the Central and Western Provinces, the present writer had been despatched to London in January, 1912, for the purpose of fully instructing the Solicitors, Messrs. Ashurst, Morris, Crisp & Co., and the services of leading counsel, Mr. Tim Healey, K.C., M.P., had been retained.

In the course of the correspondence with the Colonial Office it had been intimated that before the Secretary of State came to a decision upon the petition of the Kings and Chiefs against "The Forest Ordinance," it would be desirable to await the submission of a report by Mr. H. Conway Belfield, C.M.G.

Accordingly, Mr. Belfield arrived at Accra on February 16th, took the evidence of certain officials and others, including the Honourable the Colonial Secretary, Major Bryan, C.M.G.; the Honourable the

Attorney-General, Mr. Hudson, K.C.; the Registrar of the Supreme Court, Mr. White; the Director of Surveys, Captain Leese, R.E.; the Secretary for Native Affairs, Mr. Crowther; the Honourable Hutton-Mills, M.L.C., Barrister-at-Law; Mr. Dove, Barrister-at-Law; and Chief Mate Kole, M.L.C.; and had also the advantage of perusing a series of papers dealing with matters of land administration which it was considered desirable by the local authorities that he should see.

It is remarkable, in this connection, that no attempt was made by Mr. Belfield to interview the Kings and Chiefs of the Eastern Province, or to take their evidence. These self-same Kings and Chiefs had also presented a petition against "The Forest Ordinance"; and it is a curious fact that the local authorities did not introduce them to the Special Commissioner.

From Accra Mr. Belfield proceeded to Cape Coast, where he received a grand reception from the assembled Kings and Chiefs of the Central and Western Provinces and the Executive Committee and members of the Gold Coast Aborigines' Rights Protection Society. In replying to the address of welcome by the President of the Society, the Honourable J. P. Brown, the Special Commissioner, said :—

"I am extremely gratified to have been afforded this "opportunity of meeting you here this morning, and I "desire to say that I greatly appreciate the magnitude of "the concourse, and the signal manner in which your "welcome has been extended to me."

And again :—

"Chiefs, Elders, and Gentlemen,—I reiterate my "thanks for the cordial reception you have given to me, "and I hope that in return for the sincerity of your wel- "come I may be able to do something for your country "and yourselves."

The next day, namely, the 5th of March, was taken up by the addresses of the present writer and Mr. E. J. P. Brown, Barrister-at-Law, on behalf of the people.

After counsel had been heard, a significant question was put by the Special Commissioner, which elicited a reply which is of sufficient importance to be reproduced, particularly as it does not appear in Mr. Belfield's report, Blue Book (C.D. 6278).

" With reference to the question submitted for our con-
" sideration by you in your communication Nt. 4/12 of
" the 6th March, 1912, namely:—

" ' If all provisions authorising the Government to
" lease or otherwise appropriate Forest Reserves are
" deleted from the Bill, and if these reserves are created
" and held solely for the purpose of improving the
" forests by scientific methods, can it be shown that
" such an arrangement would be of any disadvantage to
" owners of those lands'

" We beg, on behalf of the Amanhin, Ahinfu (Kings and
" Chiefs), and the Aborigines' Society, to return the
" following reply:—

" ' The principle of conserving forests is not un-
" known to the people of this country. The Chiefs now
" and again set apart certain parts of the forest for the
" preservation of game, the collection of forest produce,
" and as sacred groves. This has been done from time
" immemorial to the present day, so that, apart from
" the timber industry and the extensive clearings made
" by the Mining Companies for fuel and timbering their
" mines, the forests of the country would be in a state
" of good preservation.'

" Therefore, we say, there is no need for a Forest Bill,
" since Native Chiefs and Kings have power under the
" Native Jurisdiction Ordinance of 1911, and in accord-
" ance with the custom and practice of the country, of
" conserving forests. The difference between the Native
" Kings and Chiefs continuing to conserve the forests in
" accordance with the native custom and the Government
" by Ordinance doing the same is this:—

" That the subjects of Native Kings and Chiefs have
" the right to the use of the land, and the act of conserving
" a given portion of the land would be the common act of
" both the Kings and Chiefs and their subjects, and,
" therefore, would cause no hardship to the subjects. On
" the other hand, upon the Government exercising the
" power of conserving forests under an Ordinance, neither
" the Kings and Chiefs, nor the subjects of their stools,
" would have a say in the matter, and the obvious result
" would be that the people would scatter through the
" consequent deprivation of their holdings and the tribal
" system would be disorganised and broken up.

" Therefore, we suggest that, instead of the Forest
" Ordinance, there should be appointed Forest In-
" structors, who will aid the Kings and Chiefs with the
" information as to how best to preserve their forests. The
" Amanhin would also be willing to give up some of their
" people to be trained for this purpose. This would be in
" accordance with the beneficent intention of the Govern-
" ment to train us in the proper economic development of
" the country.

" (Signed)   CASELY HAYFORD,
E. J. P. BROWN,

" H. Conway Belfield, Esq., C.M.G.,
" Special Commissioner,
" Cape Coast,
" March 8th, 1912."

The reader who has followed the principles of Gold
Coast land tenure will have no difficulty in appreciating the full effect of this correspondence. To a
specific question a specific answer was returned of
an all-important bearing upon " The Forest Ordinance " controversy.

From March 6th to March 9th the evidence of six
representative Chiefs of the Central and Western
Provinces and of the Honourable J. P. Brown, President of the Gold Coast Aborigines' Rights Protection
Society, Mr. T. F. E. Jones, Vice-President; Mr.
Attoh Ahuma, M.A., Secretary; Mr. Casely Hayford,
Barrister-at-Law; and Mr. E. J. P. Brown, Barrister-
at-Law, besides a statement from Mr. Furley, Commissioner of the Central Province, was taken.

The Special Commissioner arrived at Sekondi on March 10th, and evidence was taken from the following persons :—

The Provincial Commissioner, Mr. Grimshaw ;
His Honour the Senior Puisne Judge, Mr. Justice Gough ;
The Acting Solicitor-General, Mr. Adams ;
The Registrar of the Supreme Court, Mr. Vardon ;
The Manager of the Abbontiakoon Mine, Mr. Hay ;
The Manager of the Tarquah Mine, Mr. Newbury ;
The Manager of the Prestea Mine, Mr. Homersham ;
The Manager of the West African Trust Mines, Mr. Bray ;
The Paramount Chief of Bensu ;
Chief Essel Kojo of Appinto, and Mr. Giles Hunt, M.L.C.

After touring Kumasi and taking further evidence there Mr. Belfield returned to London on May 4th, and prepared his report, Blue Book (C.D. 6,278), presented to both Houses of Parliament by command of His Majesty, July, 1912, which is a marvel of industry.

2.

The Gold Coast Deputation arrived in London on the evening of Sunday, June 23rd, and took up residence at the Westminster Palace Hotel, a most convenient centre. The members thereof were Mr. T. F. E. Jones, Vice-President of the Gold Coast Aborigines' Rights Protection Society, Mr. Casely Hayford, Barrister-at-Law, Mr. E. J. P. Brown, Barrister-at-Law, and Dr. B. W. Quartey-Papafio, M.D.

It will be remembered that Mr. Belfield arrived in London on May 4th. The Deputation left the Gold Coast on the 8th of June. Between those dates, namely, on the 6th of June, 1912, Mr. Morel and his friends had got up a Deputation to wait on the Colonial Minister, praying for the appointment of a Committee " to consider the laws relating to the transfer of land in the West African Colonies and Protectorates (other than Northern Nigeria), and to report whether, if any, and if so what, amendment of the laws is required." The Colonial Minister had no difficulty in granting the prayer, and the *Times* of June 26th announced that such a Committee had been appointed, consisting of Sir Kenelm E. Digby, G.C.B., K.C.,, Chairman; Sir F. M. Hodgson, K.C.M.G., Sir W. Taylor, K.C.M.G., Mr. J. C. Wedgwood, M.P., Mr. E. D. Morel, with Mr. C. Strachey, Mr. W. D. Ellis, and Mr. R. E. Stubbs, of the Colonial Office, and Mr. H. F. Batterbee, of the Colonial Office, as Secretary.

Now, it is well-known that Mr. Morel is closely in touch with the Colonial Office. That being so, it is open to the ordinary mind to inquire whether the Colonial Office had vouchsafed him an inkling as to the purport of Mr. Belfield's report, which was not published till July, 1912. If he had been instrumental in sending Mr. Belfield out to report on the "Legislation governing the alienation of Native Lands in the Gold Coast Colony and Ashanti; with some observations on the Forest Ordinance, 1911" (C.D. 6,278), it is reasonable to suppose that he would be one of the first to be made aware of Mr. Belfield's deductions.

Now, if we recall Mr. Morel's statement that he would make use of the Press, the platform, and of Parliament to press home his policy of West African land reform, it becomes easy to understand why it was found necessary to send the letter to the *Times* of June 6th, 1912, over the signatures of Mr. E. D. Morel, Mr. Noel Buxton, Mr. J. Ramsay Macdonald, Mr. Phillip Morrell, Sir Albert Spicer, and Mr. Josiah C. Wedgwood.

The letter is of such importance that we make no apology in quoting it :—

" Sir,—The increasing importance which our West
" African dependencies are acquiring owing to the develop-
" ment of commerce and industry within them, makes it
" incumbent that the policy guiding their administration
" should be inspired by a uniform principle, whatever
" differences in application local circumstances may
" dictate. The first duty of the paramount Power is to
" give legal security to the continued native occupation
" and usage of the land.

" This principle has, so far as Northern Nigeria is con-
" cerned, now been embodied in law. The Land and
" Native Right Ordinance, 1911, establishes the three
" cardinal features of native law and custom, which, after
" careful investigation on the spot and discussion at the
" Colonial Office, was ascertained to prevail throughout
" that Protectorate. These features are:—(1) That the
" whole of the land, whether occupied or unoccupied at
" the moment, is native land—i.e., land held by the heads
" of the community in trust for that community. (2) That
" the whole of the land is controlled by the Governor, who
" through conquest has become the Paramount Chief, to
" be administered by him for the use and common benefit
" of the people of Northern Nigeria. (3) That the
" Governor's power shall be exercised in accordance with
" native law and custom.

" At the same time the Ordinance fully provides for the
" legitimate interests of European enterprises whose
" representatives on the spot obtain leases of land they
" wish to use. The rents payable for these plots is revis-
" able every seven years, under conditions which safe-
" guard the lessee against paying for increased value due
" to capital expended or to the employment of such
" capital, and which confer upon the lessee, in the event
" of a raising of the rental, the option of surrendering his
" occupancy and claiming compensation to the value of
" his inexhausted improvements.

" In Southern Nigeria, in the Gold Coast, and in Sierra
" Leone, however, the land question has not been regu-
" lated. The Government has no ultimate control over
" the land, merely exercising the right of interference
" under specified circumstances which, in the case of the
" Gold Coast and Southern Nigeria, would hardly seem
" sufficient to meet the situation which has actually arisen
" or which is threatened. Inquiries in both the Gold Coast

" and Southern Nigeria as to the character of native land
" tenure have been recently prosecuted, and reports are
" understood to be in preparation.   In Sierra Leone no
" such inquiry has been held.   From what is already
" known of the native system in these dependencies there
" is little doubt that law and custom are substantially the
" same therein as in Northern Nigeria, and it will appear
" highly desirable that the Colonial Office should examine
" how far it is expedient and practicable to extend the
" principle which has inspired the legislation of Northern
" Nigeria to these other dependencies.

" In the case of the Gold Coast especially there would
" seem to be real urgency for action, owing, on the one
" hand, to the rush for mining and agricultural con-
" cessions, and, on the other, to the widespread destruc-
" tion of valuable timbered areas.   Restricted in its
" operation by the Concessions Ordinance, due to the fore-
" sight of Mr. Joseph Chamberlain, the system permitting
" the Chiefs to grant concessions of land and forest pro-
" duce for ninety-nine years—which amounts, virtually,
" to alienation—is, nevertheless, one that, if continued,
" must trench upon the needs of the native peoples.
" Although nominally granted by the Tribal Stool—i.e.,
" by the community—there can be little doubt that in
" consenting to these transactions, usually carried out
" through the medium of native barristers from the coast,
" the Chiefs are arrogating to themselves a position with
" which they are not invested under native law and
" custom.   No native community composed of traders and
" agriculturists would knowingly alienate its sources of
" actual and potential profit.   The Gold Coast and, to
" some extent, the Ashanti people are largely composed of
" able and hard-working agriculturists, who, in recent
" years, have built up a great cocoa industry, and, even
" were it in the public interest, which we contend is not
" the case, to allow these alienations of land and of forest
" produce to continue, it is inconceivable that the native
" peoples, did they fully appreciate the matter, would be
" consenting parties to a system destructive of their own
" most vital interests.   What is required in all these, our
" tropical dependencies in West Africa, where there are no
" white settlers, are Land Acts which, however they may
" vary in their form of wording and in their application in
" accordance with the character of the political relation-
" ship prevailing between their inhabitants and the para-

" mount Power shall secure the threefold aim of legalising
" the rights of the natives to the occupancy and use of the
" soil, preventing the creation of monopolies in the soil's
" produce, whether natural or cultivated, and reserving
" the value of the land and freedom of access to it, for the
" future generations of our protected subjects.

" We venture to suggest that an experienced Committee
" might, as was done in the case of Northern Nigeria, be
" appointed by the Colonial Office to inquire into the
" problem which this letter raises, and which goes to the
" foundation of sound administration in these tropical
" regions under British protection."

As to this the Deputation sent the following reply,
which was published in the *Times* of July 18th. Other
correspondence relating to this will be found in the
appendix :—

"Sir,—We arrived here from the Gold Coast on a depu-
" tation to the Colonial Office upon the Forest Bill, 1911,
" on the 23rd ult., and our attention has been called to
" a letter in *The Times* of June 6, under the heading
" ' West African Land : British Policy and Native Rights,'
" above the signatures of Mr. E. D. Morel, Mr. Noel
" Buxton, Mr. J. Ramsay Macdonald, Mr. Phillip Morrel,
" Sir Albert Spicer, and Mr. Josiah C. Wedgwood.

" As the recommendations made in this letter would
" seriously conflict with the customary rights of the people
" of the Gold Coast over their lands, and break the entire
" social system and tribal organisation, we deem it our
" duty to venture an explanation.

" It may not be generally known that in the year 1897
" a Lands Bill was introduced in the Gold Coast Legisla-
" ture, the result of which would have been, had the Bill
" received the Royal Assent, to practically transfer to the
" Crown from the rightful owners lands which the Crown
" could claim neither by right of conquest nor cession nor
" by purchase.

" A deputation representing the united opinion of the
" natives in opposition to the Bill was sent to England,
" and was received by Mr. Joseph Chamberlain, the then
" Secretary of State for the Colonies. The objections to
" that Bill, which are identical with the objections now
" put forward to the Forest Bill, 1911, were contained in

" a petition presented to the Colonial Office through
" Messrs. Ashurst, Morris, Crisp, and Co.

" Mr. Chamberlain then acknowledged that the objec-
" tions raised against the Bill were well founded, and the
" Bill never became law, but in the result the Concessions
" Ordinance, 1900, was passed.

" Now, the Forest Bill, 1911, having in substance the
" same effect on the proprietary rights of the people as
" the Lands Bill of 1897, the Kings and Chiefs of the
" Western and Central Provinces of the Gold Coast com-
" municated with the Secretary of State for the Colonies,
" asking that their representatives be given an opportunity
" of laying before His Majesty in Council their petition.

" Counsel on behalf of the Kings and Chiefs and the
" people were also subsequently heard in the Legislative
" Council of the Gold Coast upon the Bill, when the
" Governor assured them that their arguments would
" receive consideration.

" As a result, the Secretary of State for the Colonies
" appointed Mr. H. Conway Belfield, C.M.G., as a Special
" Commissioner to the Gold Coast to report upon the sub-
" ject, and counsel were heard by Mr. Belfield, and the
" latter subsequently took privately the evidence of
" several prominent persons.

" To deal briefly with the suggestions of Mr. Morel and
" his friends, we find the following propositions stated as
" to land tenure in Northern Nigeria, namely:—

" (1) ' That the whole of the land, whether occupied
" or unoccupied at the moment, is native land—i.e., land
" held by the heads of the community in trust for that
" community.'

" (2) ' That the whole of the land is controlled by the
" Governor, who through conquest has become the para-
" mount Chief to be administered by him for the use and
" common benefit of the people of Northern Nigeria.'

" (3) ' That the Governor's power shall be exercised in
" accordance with native law and custom.'

" The first part of the above proposition (1) requires no
" affirmation, as it is incontrovertible that in the case of
" the lands of the Gold Coast they have belonged to the
" people from time immemorial, and no legislation is

" necessary to this end. The second part of the proposi-
" tion cannot apply to the Gold Coast as a correct state-
" ment of the customary relationship between heads of
" communities and the members thereof, since, according
" to native law, a Chief is a joint owner with his people,
" and he cannot exercise any proprietary rights without
" the co-operation of his people.

" The proposition (2) is wholly inapplicable to the Gold
" Coast, since the Crown has never laid claim to acquisi-
" tion of the lands of the country either by conquest,
" cession, or purchase.

" Proposition (3) is also obviously superfluous.

" It is seriously suggested in the letter under reply that
" Northern Nigeria land laws should be extended to the
" Gold Coast. This cannot be, for the circumstances are
" wholly different, as anyone who has taken the trouble to
" study the facts must acknowledge. We take leave also
" to point out that the ' real urgency for action ' on the
" Gold Coast suggested by Mr. Morel and his friends was
" likewise urged in 1897 in the case of the ' Lands Bill,'
" and Mr. Chamberlain, after mature consideration,
" arrived at the conclusion that such a Bill was not desir-
" able.

" The fact is conceded that a great cocoa industry has
" been built up by the industry of able and hard-working
" Gold Coast and Ashanti native agriculturists, and if the
" object of Mr. Morel and his friends is to secure the
" economic development of the Gold Coast under condi-
" tions which would work no hardship on the native
" African and leave his institutions intact, we would ven-
" ture to suggest that the petition of the Kings and Chiefs
" of the people of the Gold Coast should receive their
" serious support.

" Your obedient servants,
" T. F. E. JONES,
" CASELY HAYFORD,
" E. J. P. BROWN,
" B. W. QUARTEY-PAPAFIO, M.D.,
" Natives, Members of the Deputa-
" tion appointed by the Kings and
" Chiefs of the Gold Coast to oppose
" the Forest Bill, 1911.

" The Westminster Palace Hotel, Victoria Street, S.W.,
" July 4."

From the foregoing it will occur to the intelligent reader that a grave danger threatens the West African Dependencies in their political life.   We refer to the danger of their destinies being ruled by party politics rather than by any settled scientific policy.

Mr. Wedgwood, a Labour Member of the House of Commons, and one of the devotees of land nationalisation in West Africa, states in an article in the October number of the *African Times and Orient Review*, which is but a reproduction of the same article noticed in an earlier chapter, that the policy advocated may some time be seen to apply to England also.   It may be open to question whether compulsory socialism will usher in the Millennium. The danger, in any case, is apparent.   It is possible for Colonial Office policy to be controlled by the views of the supporters of the Government who are strong enough to press the same home and make it inconvenient for the Colonial Office to ignore them.   It is no wonder that practical men are beginning to question whether party government works for the   efficiency of the British Empire.   Lord Rosebery, writing in the December, 1912, issue of *The Review of Reviews*, says :—

" The fact is that party is an evil—perhaps even prob-
" ably a necessary evil, but still an evil.   It is the curse of
" our country that so many, especially in high places,
" should worship it as a god.   It has become so much a
" part of our lives that even those who think ill of it think
" it as inevitable as the fog ; so inevitable that it is of no
" use thinking what we should do without it.   And yet its
" operation blights efficiency."

Of the internal work of the Deputation I am not free to speak at present.   It is enough to say that they were received at the Colonial Office on the morning of June 28th by the Right Honourable Lewis Harcourt, His Majesty's Secretary of State to the Colonies, and were introduced by Mr. Tim Healey,

K.C., M.P., in a masterly and telling speech, instructed by Messrs. Ashurst, Morris, Crisp and Co., the well-known London solicitors. It is to be hoped that later will be published in a Blue Book form the proceedings, including Mr. Healey's speech and the speeches of the members of the Deputation, and the same presented to both Houses of Parliament.

It is open to say that the Deputation (who were supported by the Rev. W. R. Griffin, Chairman of the Wesleyan Mission, Gold Coast, the Rev. Dr. Hayford, of the Baptist Mission, Gold Coast, and Mr. J. M. A. Oppon), were received by Mr. Harcourt with marked courtesy and sympathy. Up to the time of writing no official pronouncement has been made upon the points urged upon the attention of the Colonial Minister by Mr. Healey and the members of the Deputation. Meanwhile, the West African Land Committee continues its sittings, and, it is said, that the answer to the prayer of the Deputation will depend upon the report of the said Committee.

The Deputation returned to the Gold Coast on the 19th of September, 1912, impressed by the kindness of prominent statesmen, journalists, and publicists, including Sir Norval Helme, M.P., Mr. Alfred Stead, Editor of the *Review of Reviews*, Sir William McGeary, Mr. Hayes Redwar, and others, and with a keen appreciation of the able services of Mr. Healey, K.C., M.P., and the solicitors, Messrs. Ashurst, Morris, Crisp, and Co.

3.

Meanwhile, affairs were moving in the sister Dependency of Southern Nigeria. Reuter's cablegram of August 8th contained the following :—

" The Chiefs and people of Abeokuta, including a large
" number of farmers of different sections of the country,
" waited upon the Alake to-day for an explanation with
" regard to rumours that the Government intended to
" deprive them of the ownership of their land.

" The Alake invited the British Commissioner, who was
" present, to make a statement, and the latter said that
" he could not believe that it was the intention of the
" Government to deprive them of the ownership of their
" lands. The multitude subsequently departed somewhat
" consoled, but the farmers have been greatly disturbed
" by the rumours."

It is idle to suggest, as has been done in leading
articles in the *African Mail*, that the objection of
the people of Southern Nigeria to the land policy of
the Government had been induced by the " mendaci-
ties " of the Gold Coast Press. It is also wrong.
For the suggestion is misleading; and no one with
first-hand acquaintance with West Africa could possibly make the mistake. The alarm on the Gold Coast
was immediately caused by " The Forest Bill." The
unrest in Southern Nigeria was due to " The Foreshore Case." According to the deputation which
waited upon the Acting Governor on June 13, 1912,
" the continuance of the publication in several issues
of the Government Gazettes since the 20th of September, 1911, of a Public Notice informing the
general public of a decision of the FULL COURT which
sat at Lagos on the 22nd of April last year over " THE
FORESHORE CASE " is indeed causing great consterna-
tion and unrest among the Natives of all classes in this
community."

Both " The Forest Bill " and " The Foreshore
Case " publications aimed at the extension of the
principle of the Northern Nigerian Land proclamation. That principle aimed at the final control of the
people's lands by the Crown. It was unlikely that
people either in the Gold Coast, or in Southern

Nigeria, would not raise a protest. Mr. Belfield, in his report, has admitted the genuineness of the protest of the Gold Coast. Acting Governor Mr. James must have been forced to admit that our Southern Nigerian brethren had made out a strong case. The nature of the case made out has already been indicated in an earlier chapter, and, as we are writing, there is a deputation on its way to the Colonial Office from Southern Nigeria to lay the facts before the Departmental Committee.

Again, on the arrival of Sir Frederick Lugard in Lagos, a deputation waited upon him on February 28th to urge, among others, objections to the land policy of the Government. They were explicit upon the matter. " The deputation prayed that His Majesty's Government clearly define the rights of the British Crown to legislate for the countries in Yoruba, before undertaking any legislation upon the lands of the people. The various constituencies of what is known as Yoruba entered into compact with the British Government voluntarily and of their own accord. There was a cession as in the case of Lagos, treaties of commerce as in the case of Abeokuta, treaties of friendship as in the case Ibadan, treaties for the abolition of human sacrifice as in the case of Ilesha and Ode Ondo, etc., etc., and nothing more. It was understood and distinctly stipulated that these communities are responsible for the management of their internal affairs. It was necessary, therefore, before any legislation on land tenure is experimented upon, that the Government define the rights under which it proposes to legislate.''

It is important to record these facts. They tend to show that West Africa is in earnest over this land question, and that it is idle to think that the unrest is without foundation.

4.

While the deputation was in England, the retire-
ment of Mr. Thorburn from the administration of the
Gold Coast and the appointment of Sir Hugh Charles
Clifford to take up the reins of government were announced in the *Times.*   Since then the new
Governor has arrived, and has succeeded in impres-
sing the community favourably.   There is an element
of strength in the new Governor's character; and
it is reasonable to hope that a new era is about dawn-
ing in the history of the Gold Coast.   We only trust
that the local man will give him a chance.   For if,
like Sissyphus, we have hitherto rolled up the burden
of our political needs only to rebound at our feet, it
has been due, to a large extent, to the manipulation of
the man on the spot.   The man on the spot is useful.
He is even indispensable.   But he has his limitations.
He is generally devoid of imagination.   He gets into
a rut and sticks there.   And God knows West African
administration wants nothing so much at present as
robust imagination, quickening sympathy, and sober
good sense.   It was a man of strong character and
ripe experience who wrote with reference to the
Sierra Leone hut tax :—

" Let the causes of irritation be removed and endeavour
" be made by every means to restore the confidence which
" has been destroyed or grievously shaken.   Let the
" colonial officers, from the very highest to the lowest sub-
" ordinate, realise that the subjects of a protectorate have
" rights, and that it should be a work of forbearance and
" patience, rather than of overpowering force, to instruct
" them that they also have obligations and duties towards
" the protecting power.   Let government be on fixed
" principles of justice, not by haphazard opportunism.
" Let the chiefs be restored to their places in the country,
" a wise supervision being exercised over them, with a
" minimum of interference, and the substitution being
" encouraged of agricultural and other industries for idle-

" ness or tribal or personal contests.   Let the civilising
" influences of well-directed missionary teaching be also
" encouraged.   Let wise and sympathetic government be
" the primary object, and we may be assured that, with
" the gradual raising of the level of civilisation and the
" increase of population and of industry, which such
" government will bring with it, revenue for all needs will
" follow, whilst endeavours to compel revenue by short-
" sighted and unsuitable means must inevitably result in
" failure."*

* Parliamentary Papers, C.9, 388.

CHAPTER VII.

THE LESSONS OF THE WESTERN TOUR.

There is yet a phase of colonial administration that awaits to commend itself to the statesmanship of the civilised world. Lord Rosebery has recently drawn attention to Japan as an object-lesson in national efficiency. It appears that in colonial administration also she can hold a candle to the foremost nations of the earth. And her secret lies in applying natural laws to the line of development of a given dependency.

According to Baron Goto, Japan, in dealing with Formosa, aimed at " a policy of pacification, not extermination; of illumination, not punishment," with the phenomenal success which has astounded the world. ' Illumination '—that is a good word. It pre-figures light. It suggests chasing darkness out of every crevice of Formosan nationality. It connotes bringing the ruled to the level of the opportunity of the rulers. ' Pacification '—that is another good word. It implies harmonious relations between the government and the governed. It excludes any possibility of exploitation. It encourages confidence. It presents a hope that casts out fear.

If a leaf might be taken from Japan's book in British West African colonial administration, it would stand to reason that a system would be mapped out from which would be eliminated any idea of " extermination " or " punishment." It is far from being suggested that either in Ashanti, or in Northern Nigeria, the idea of extermination or punishment enters into the mind of the Administration. But when you come to look more deeply into things, it will be discovered that much that is possible in either of the two places would not occur, were not the heel of the conqueror, theoretically at least, on the neck of the conquered. For that reason the forward movement involved in the Formosan experiment might well engage the serious attention of the Colonial Office.

And yet years and years ago, in the days of merchant rule under Governor Maclean, familiarly known to Gold Coast people as " Badayi," he indicated to Great Britain some such policy as the Formosan one. I have described this before, and will describe and contrast it again in the same words :—

" The obtuseness, in certain respects of the British " Adminstration, since Governor Maclean's death, has " been something amazing. That far-seeing man saw " through it all, and framed his policy accordingly. He " understood that the business of the Administration was " not that of unduly interfering with the internal affairs " of the protected people, and, therefore, sought to con- " solidate and strengthen Native Authority. What is " more, he perceived that England's true interest in the " Gold Coast was to make it an open market through " which the trade of the hinterland might pass freely. " Therefore, without over-estimating his authority or his " strength, by conciliation and moral persuasion he en- " couraged the Ashantis to come down freely to the open " market of the Gold Coast, guaranteeing them safety by " prevailing on the Fantis to be on their good behaviour. " In his mental vista, he beheld a prosperous Gold " Coast, with Ashanti, as a great emporium of trade, " interchanging with and pouring into the lap of the Gold " Coast the rich resources and products of that now " blasted land. He encouraged and was instrumental in " the training in England of the Princes Quantamissa and " Osoo Ansah, to be the medium of intelligent influence " in the hinterland ; and who, having the slightest ac- " quaintance with Gold Coast history, can say that the " late Prince Osoo Ansah did not do his best to bring about " a permanent friendly understanding, in his day, between

" Ashanti and the Gold Coast? It was a policy full of
" common sense and practical statesmanship. It was the
" work of the Colonial Office, in recent years, to have
" struck at Governor Maclean's work, root and branch, by
" attempting to discredit, but without success, the sons
" of the late Prince Ansah in the eyes of their countrymen
" and the British public.

" A different policy was that of Sir Charles Macarthy,
" another British Governor, who flourished, as far as the
" Gold Coast is concerned, in the first quarter of the nine-
" teenth century. He also saw in the distance, but saw
" differently. He was deeply conscious of the power of
" England—a power which, he considered, no subject race
" could withstand ; and he was impatient of what seemed
" an impediment in the way of England's aggrandise-
" ment in these parts. If he could only pierce into the
" interior, what untold treasures would not be open to
" England to gather in? In this spirit he, the faithful
" servant of the Crown, went forth with drawn sword,
" breaking down the power of the Chiefs, and subduing
" all before it. Impatient of obstacles, he was also im-
" patient of counsel as to the best way to overcome such
" obstacles. Accordingly, he went forth in the faith and
" in the strength of the conqueror, seeking new territories
" which should own allegiance to Great Britain through
" his prowess. He considered the kingdom of Ashanti a
" barrier to British commerce and enterprise piercing the
" interior, and he fondly wished to see that barrier
" down. He tried to break through, and died in the
" attempt."

Sir Hugh Clifford, the new Governor of the Gold
Coast, arrived in the Dependency on December 26th,
1912, and has already made a successful tour through
the Eastern Province. Even now the merest tyro
can feel that a strong personality is at the helm of
affairs. It is also felt that a blow has been dealt at
the old attitude of *laissez-faire* by the new Administration, and that if the evil again rears its head in
the history of the country, it will be the fault of the
Colonial Office. All honest men are uniting in wishing
for the present Administration long life, enduring
record, and unbounded success.

His Excellency landed at Seccondee on the 18th of April, 1913, and began his tour of the Western Province. He succeeded in making a favourable impression all round, and his intercourse with the people was marked with courtesy and tact. Only the man on the spot seemed somewhat nervous. Hitherto petty officers, in their zeal for the Crown, had thought, and, in some cases, demanded that Native Rulers of the first order should lower their apparel and bare their trunks before them. The people resented this as an act of humiliation. Would the new Administration perpetuate the affront, or show proper regard for the self-respect of the very persons whose frank co-operation is necessary in an effort to govern the country successfully? Hence the anxiety of the petty officer and the local man. The new Governor took natural law for his guide. He recognised the fact that if you wish to enlist the sympathy, the confidence, and the esteem of a people, you must begin by showing regard for their self-respect and self-esteem. It might be said it was the simple act of a gentleman. We want badly real gentlemen in His Majesty's West African Civil Service. It would be half the solution of the administrative problem.

We have said the local man was nervous. He had always represented the educated African almost as a rogue and a vagabond. Would that aspect wear with a strong personality capable of sifting facts for himself?

The phenomenon of the educated native and the part he may play in colonial administration is not confined to British waters. It invades our friends the Germans. It appears that German colonial opinion has a tendency to regard it as being to the interest of German colonial expansion not to encourage the cultivation of knowledge on the part of the Native. It is fair to point out that this tendency is not encouraged by the Kaiser's Government.   Any way, from the standpoint of German colonial opinion to Mr. Morel's suggestion in his recent article on " Native Medical Men and the West African Colonial Service," that Native barristers should be confined to the coast towns, there is a great leap, so prodigious as to make comparison seem to argue the absence of a sense of proportion.   Still, in essentials, the objection in either case is based on the same principle.   That principle, in its last analysis, is a desire to keep the Native in his place. Force of circumstances have made Mr. Morel's " coast barrister " what he is. He is an inconvenient entity.   It is suggested that in German territories no Native has yet shown a capacity for intellectual attainments that would attract the German world.   If so, it is a pity.   But I should like, all the same, to place in the hands of the German Emperor and German pro-Consuls the thought-moving works of the late Dr. Edward Wilmot Blyden.   I am sure German psychologists and scientists will appreciate Edward Wilmot Blyden. They will recognise in him a kindred soul, and he may help to correct German colonial opinion.   I should like to see in wide circulation in German states and territories " The African Times and Orient Review."   The world has need of teaching.   How can men know unless they are told?   And some day wise men will realise that God has made of one blood all nations of the earth to dwell therein, and that all are illumined by the same spirit, the spirit of vision and understanding.

Yet may it be said that, so long as the mothers and the wives and the sisters of the bulk of the people remain true to Africa, there will never be wanting mine-hands or tillers of the fields.   Hence there is no need to stay the hand of progress in other directions.   Nature must have way.   And if you attempt to stop her, she may overwhelm you with disaster.

It is obvious that Sir Hugh Clifford will have his
work cut out in trying to reach the people and to
understand them first-hand. It will not be his fault if
he is baffled. It will not even be the fault of the local
man. It will be the fault of a system that in the
past has seen nothing, known nothing, save through
the eyes of the local man. That system must be
broken. Our Governors hitherto have not governed.
They have not been in touch with the people. They
have been occasional travelling inspectors of a magnificent order. From Accra to Seccondee, Seccondee
to Coomassie and back, has been the rôle. We have
reason to believe that Sir Hugh is too great not to
seek to reach the root of things for himself. In this
he will prove another Maclean in Gold Coast annals
—a man who even in these degenerate days can rule
this Dependency through the natural rulers by the
magic wand of sheer sympathy, firmness, courtesy
and a robust imagination.

Sir Frederick Lugard will, at the same time, in
the sister Dependency, we have reason to hope, so
shape things that, although in Northern Nigeria men
are said to prostrate themselves before officialdom,
it will not end in a prostration of the national soul,
and that in him there is a possibility of a United
West Africa raising its head among the nations to
bless the memory of a great pro-Consul.

Meanwhile it is believed that whatever crisis arises
in the West African situation, there will be men ready
to cope with it, and to lead the people aright.

CHAPTER VIII.

THE SIGNIFICANCE OF THE CAPE COAST VISIT.

Following closely upon the Western tour was the Governor's visit to Cape Coast. His Excellency landed there on the morning of Thursday, May 15, 1913, and great was the ovation. Never before within the writer's experience had a Governor of the Gold Coast been received by the people with such enthusiasm. It was an unique occasion, and every circumstance lent force to the result of the supreme moment.

Whisperings of Sir Hugh Clifford's career in other parts of the Empire had gone before him. But the people were yet to judge for themselves the manner of man he was. And they have been quick to discern in him a sincerity of purpose, a breadth of outlook, and sympathetic consideration which are bound to enlist their co-operation in the Administration.

He has told us plainly that we are not to expect him to create for us a new heaven and a new earth. That was good. That was frank. But that very frankness has enabled the people to feel that whatever is possible for the happiness and the good of the many will find in him an initiative and a support.

Here were assembled at Cape Coast to meet His Excellency all the leading Amanhin and Ahinfu (Kings and Chiefs) of the Central Province. And the warmth and the manner of the reception could hardly be eclipsed elsewhere in the British Empire. Cape

Coast is the seat of the Gold Coast Aborigines' Rights Protection Society, and delegates from the Axim and the Accra branches had come all the way down to join in the reception. Between the enthusiasm of the Amanhin and Ahinfu, the local officials, the Aborigines' Society, and the general mass of the people, such a meeting of the Governor and representatives of the governed has been recorded as might safely go down to posterity in the annals of the Gold Coast.

The Gold Coast Aborigines' Rights Protection Society was founded in the troublous times of the Lands Bill, and a deputation thereof was received by Mr. Chamberlain, the Colonial Minister, at Downing Street, in 1898, and accorded a satisfactory and a favourable hearing in the matter of the Lands Bill. At its inauguration the Society had received the warm congratulations of Governor Hodgson. Mr. Belfield, in his report, has found favourably as to its financial position and prestige in the country. That it ranks high in the estimation of the people may be gathered from the fact that the prominent members thereof are connected, in most cases, with reigning houses in the country. The late King Ghartey of Winnebah, on his dying bed, sent a message to the Society, and that was, "Be constitutional." He was a man of ripe judgment and political sagacity, whose memory is held in high esteem. It is no wonder that the leaders of the people have always been on the side of loyal but firm representation of the grievances of the country, and it is equally no wonder that the Aborigines' Society has always received due recognition on the part of His Majesty's Government. It is also no wonder that His Excellency, Sir Hugh Clifford, has been so favourably impressed with the work of the Society as to have referred to it in his speech at the banquet given by the Society in his honour as "your great Society."

The Gold Coast Aborigines' Rights Protection Society requires no charter of incorporation. It is an indigenous growth which must flourish for all time, much as the system by which our Amanhin and Ahinfu flourish. It is the National Assembly of the people, where their enlightened sons meet with the Kings and Chiefs as one deliberative body in the interests of the people. The foundations upon which it is based and the principles by which it is worked are in accordance with the accepted principles of native institutions. As such it is of happy augury that the relations between the Government and the Society are so cordial, and that easy and frank co-operation are ensured.

His Excellency must have been impressed with the exceptional educational work that is being carried on at Cape Coast. He must have visited the new building works of the Wesleyan Mission under the energetic direction of the Rev. W. R. Griffin, the head of the Mission, and learnt the history of the Richmond College and Mfantsipim school. He must have heard with a degree of interest that the Mission spends some £10,000 a year on educational work, for which the Government returns them only about £1,000. He must have visited the Catholic Mission, and witnessed the new Technical Institute, which is in process of building, and he must also have noticed the good work that is being done by the Sisters in the training of girls. His Excellency's attention must have been drawn to the equally interesting educational developments of the S.P.G. with a Grammar School under the management of a highly trained man. And we know that he found time even to have visited the primary schools of the Zion Church and others. Surely, with all this going on at Cape Coast, and brought to the Governor's notice, he must have come away with the impression that this is the intellectual centre of the Gold Coast.

What Cape Coast wants, and wants badly, is a return of its quondam prosperity. That is neither to be coaxed by fine phrases nor fair promises. The situation has to be faced, and faced squarely. It was roundly stated by Governor Rodger in 1907. Said he :—

" Since my arrival at Cape Coast I have heard a good deal about trade depression ; and I fear that complaints on this subject are not altogether unfounded. Now that Coomassie has become an important trading centre, and that a railway line connects Coomassie with the port of Seccondee, you can never again expect to have the same practical monopoly of Ashanti trade that you enjoyed in the past, but you should face these facts with courage and resolution, and determine to replace such positions of the Hinterland trade as you may have lost by the development of other resources. I have already suggested increased cultivation of cocoa in the richer planting districts of the interior, and you should also plant cotton, sugar-cane, and maize, and improve and extend your plantation of oil-palm and kola-nuts.

Another very valued resource consists in the development of trade in rubber and timber. Within the boundaries of this Province extensive forests containing both these products are available ; and planting existing supplies might be largely increased. Then, in the immediate neighbourhood of Cape Coast, you might breed poultry, and other live stock and grow fruits and vegetables, to supply the ships calling at this port as well as the local market ; while a fruit trade especially in bananas and pineapples, might be established with Europe in the same manner as has proved so beneficial in the coast of West Indies. I know that you have difficulties of transport to contend with, and that you have few, if any roads, in this Province suitable for wheeled traffic ; but you might make more barrels, as is so largely done in the Eastern Province, for rolling your produce down from the interior, and I hope to improve and extend your road system during the year 1908.

If planting development warrants the necessary expenditure, a Government Railway should eventually be constructed to connect with Cape Coast, and the planting districts of the interior, similar to the line which is about to be constructed for Accra."

(Extract from the Government Gazette (Extraordinary), No. 40, Page 464, dated 29th June, 1907.)

Since then we know that considerable planting of cocoa has been going on at the back of Cape Coast and Elmina, and there is a suggestion of a line being extended within a distance of twenty-four miles from Cape Coast. Private companies may, or may not, find it profitable to approach the Government to be allowed to build connecting lines. But it is within the power of enterprising business men to force the hands of the Government by such an increase in the agricultural output which cannot be ignored. Nor must we put all our eggs into one basket. Even in the immediate neighbourhood of Cape Coast can lemons, oranges, pineapples, and such like products be grown to the lasting good of this ancient and historic town. The people are full of commonsense, and they must have grasped the argument which seems to tell against an immediate prospect of Cape Coast being connected with the main line. But, given the feasibility of Elmina as a good natural harbour and the agricultural developments that are reasonably anticipated, an ideal connection of Cape Coast with the main line will be through Gwikwa, Manpon, and on to Imbraim, where it would meet the trunk line. We know the question of transport will engage the first attention of the present enlightened Administration; and though, for the moment, it may be somewhat remote, let us hope that before very long it will be possible to have such a system of railway development which will make it easy for a business man to get from one end of the country to the other in reasonable time. The Governor has invited the opinion and the advice of competent persons on the matter, and all must co-operate in bringing about the desired end.

CHAPTER IX.

THE FUTURE OF WEST AFRICA.*

The future of West Africa demands that the youth of West Africa should start life with a distinct objective. Of brain power we are assured. Of mechanical skill there is no dearth. What is wanted is the directing hand which will point to the right goal.

Energy is a fine thing. But force let loose may involve itself and others in disaster. As in the mechanical world so in the national life.

I bring to you this day a message of hope. One touch of nature has made all West Africa kin. The common danger to our ancestral lands has made us one—one in danger, one in safety. United we stand, divided we fall. This may fittingly be said to your elders. More fittingly should it appeal to you. In your school and college life, with modern facilities, you have those elements present which should make intelligent co-operation easy. He is but a poor observer who does not see that there is a time coming when one policy shall guide all the Governments of the West African Dependencies. He is no lover of his country, he is no guide to his people, who does not realise that West Africa's salvation entirely depends upon a clear conception of her place within the British Empire.

---

* The first part of this chapter was originally an address by the writer, delivered (*in absentia*) to the scholars of the New High Class School, Lagos; and it is here adopted that it may reach a wider circle of West Africans.

All this, you may say, has nothing to do with the youth of West Africa. If the future of the fatherland is in your keeping, then it has everything to do with you. The time has gone past when our curriculum may follow any type. We should study science with particular application to the needs of West Africa. In history we should seek for tests to promote the healthy evolution of the people.

Africa will always be Africa both in Church and State, and the sooner practical men appreciate that fact the better. The methods of the pioneers of civilisation among us were peculiar. They were even dangerous. They tended to destroy African nationality. There was no hope for such as once entered its portals. That some are escaping, that the national conscience is being aroused, is certainly the work of the immortals.

There is, indeed, work for men and gods. For who can change the dual man? It is hard enough to direct aright the unspoilt man. But the task becomes doubly hard where you have to bring order out of two warring elements in one human breast. That is the legacy that the earlier methods of approaching the untutored African has left us. The fathers have eaten sour grapes, and the children's teeth are set on edge. Who shall deliver us from the body of this death?

I bid you wake, even the youths of West Africa, and apply this lesson unto your hearts. The future is with you. It demands that you should be up and doing. I would quicken in you thought. I would inspire in you the love of country above all things. I would deepen in you reverence for the old. I would dispel the tendency to forsake the tried way of life of our forbears. The death premium in West Africa to-day is very high. The most promising are cut off in the prime of life. There is a wasting disease which eats away the vitals of your promising sons. It is the canker of care which is bred of forcing ourselves into alien ways of life. It is that which will prevent us from giving a good account of ourselves unto God and man.

For a change, I should give a prize to the youth who would contribute an idea to the solution of the race problem. To the individualistic soul who would dare to do amid the jeers and taunts of his fellowmen; who would endure crucifixion for an idea, I would raise a monument of imperishable glory. I would canonise him upon whose shoulders is borne the people's burden of vague complaint and murmur. And I would search for such among the very youths whom I have the honour of addressing.

We want thinkers, thinkers of great thoughts. We want leaders, born leaders of men. To what good is all your learning if you cannot help us in the day of our need? You cannot think great thoughts in Africa by adopting wholesale the hurry and the bustle and the way of life of the European. Nature did not intend it. Those who attempt it end in trouble. Nay, worse. It means death. For even the dual man cannot serve both God and Mammon. And no worse burden could be imposed by civilisation on African nationality than the burden of the double life, the arch-enemy of Truth.

Shakespeare has said :

" This above all, to thine own self be true,
And it must follow as the night the day,
Thou canst not then be false to any man."

And the universal conscience of man must endorse this testimony. *Non*conformity is a great thing. It requires a man of character to be true unto himself. Anyone can conform. It needed a Martin Luther to lead the spirit of revolt. John Wesley was certainly greater than the uninteresting Oxford dons of his day. The spirit of protest sets thinking men upon enquiry. Jesus Christ was the greatest *non-conformist* the world has seen. We want badly in West Africa the spirit of honest protest. We want personalities who will dare to lead the people back to real life. It is unpopular work. But, then, great souls have never run after popularity. The first duty of every thinking African, then, is to aim at truth in the life of the people which is the basis of national consciousness. There is no reason why " the grace of manner and the charm of speech " should not be ours. But we miss the high mark of our national calling when we elect to be puppets in soul at the bidding of alien formulæ.

Are there men on whom we can rely in the work of national and racial emancipation? If not, where can we find them, where can we rear them? If in your cricket and football teams, or other manly exercises, you cannot prepare yourselves in that element of self-reliance, then is our future dark. We should like to feel that one tocsin call can arouse West Africa into national consciousness. What is it that bridges creeds and dogmas, tribes and prejudices, as broad culture? If we cannot find breadth of outlook, lofty patriotism, in our schools and colleges, where else shall we find them? Therefore, again, must you apply the lesson to your hearts that the future is with you.

When you leave school, a calling in life will engage your attention. There is far too much of the Government clerical desk and the merchant's counting house to do us any good as a race. Strike out for yourselves. Strike out boldly and on original lines. Then will the future of West Africa be assured. The gentle soul can win its way through life. Be as wise as serpents and gentle as doves. There is no need for race antagonisms. And if such there must be, prove that by your superior culture such considerations are beneath you. To you manhood should be all important, no matter by what outward symbol differentiated. For "A man's a man for a' that." And sooner or later that truth will be forced upon wise men.

There are Japanese business houses in London. I have seen shops in London where Australian and New Zealand wares and raw materials are exhibited. Why may there not be West African business houses and agencies in the United Kingdom? Let us be up and doing; combine all you can. Let dreamers dream and workers work. But whether you think or work, your country calls upon you to give the best of your brain power.

I bring you this day, and, through you, the universal youth of West Africa, a message of hope. I bring you also a message of goodwill. I bid you shake hands across the waters over your common need, your common trouble, your common anxiety. And what I say to you I say to your elders. I would ask you in the language of the "Song of Hiawatha" to smoke the peace pipe together. It is a sacrament to be received on bended knees. And United West Africa rises chastened and stimulated by the thought that in union is her strength, her weakness in discord.

2.

Again the future of West Africa demands that her sons should have a due appreciation of her place within the British Empire. There will be no harm either in Great Britain recognising her value and assigning her due recognition.

In that admirable work, " The True Temper of Empire," by Sir Charles Bruce, whose writings on Imperial questions teem with so much good sense, we are shown the value of the tropical Dependencies to Great Britain.   He tells us that " The international struggle for the control of the tropics has brought home to us that no aggregation of nations in temperate zones can constitute a self-sufficing and self-contained Empire.   It has forced us to realise the extent to which the great staples of the world's commerce come, not from the temperate regions, but from the tropics."   He quotes for us a contribution to this point from the objects of the British Cotton Growing Association as set out in the prospectus in these words : " It has been estimated that if all the cotton mills in this country were running three-quarter time instead of full time, the loss would be not less than £300,000 a week, or at the rate of £15,000,000 per annum."

Someone may say that these are obvious truths. But truths have a fashion of not appearing until some directing hand points to them.   And so even now it is necessary to urge that the place of West Africa and her importance to the life of the Empire are not sufficiently appreciated.   The *African Mail*, in a terse leading article in the issue of March 21, 1913, bemoans the situation.   It treats us to facts and figures of an interesting order.   It says :—

" How great is the comparative importance of British " West Africa in relation to the other dependencies of the " Crown is a fact but too often lost sight of even in these " days.   In area, in population, and in natural wealth—if " we except mineral wealth, and we shall not be able to " make that exception for very much longer—the West " African Dependencies are, in combination, incomparably " the most important of our tropical and semi-tropical " sphere of Imperial activity.   Their administration is " really the biggest task which faces the Colonial Office.   It " is the biggest responsibility which the nation has incurred

" in the government of the subject races—India, of course,
" excepted. That is not understood by the general public.
" And yet it is an unquestionable fact. The total area of
" British West Africa is 444,342 square miles, just short
" of being four times the area of the United Kingdom,
" within 30,000 square miles of the area covered by the
" South African Union, larger than the two Rhodesias,
" twice the size of the Uganda Protectorate and East
" Africa Protectorate respectively, two-thirds as large as
" Bechuanaland with Basutoland and Swaziland thrown in.
" But when we turn to populations, the relative import-
" ance of British West Africa is still more significant.
" British West Africa numbers 20,176,635, while the South
" African Union numbers only 5,973,394 (white and
" coloured included), Rhodesia 1,593,676, Uganda 2,843,325,
" East Africa 2,651,892. In fact, the whole of British
" Africa, other than West Africa, consisting of the South
" African Union, Basutoland, Swaziland, Bechuanaland,
" Rhodesia, Nyasaland, Uganda, East Africa, and Somali-
" land only numbers a total of 15,043,503 inhabitants against
" British West Africa's 20,176,635. British West Africa
" is also the most densely populated part of British Africa,
" the average being 45.4 (in Southern Nigeria the average is
" 98.4) per square mile, against 12.6 in the territories of
" the South African Union, 12.7 in Uganda, 10.2 in East
" Africa, 3.6 in Rhodesia, and so on. A proper apprecia-
"tion of these facts is required to give to British West
"Africa the place to which it is entitled in the public mind."

These things being so, West Africa calls for a
treatment suitable to her condition. And the first
thing which she may reasonably demand is efficiency
in her service. If her importance is hardly second
to that of India, it is only fair that her servants
should be about as good. There is only one way
of rendering the Civil Service efficient. That is by
competitive examination. It should be an examination open to all, irrespective of creed, colour, or
prejudice. It should be a test in which the best
brains would win. The candidates should be known
by numbers, not names, to avoid the possibility of
sympathy or favour. And the spoils of office should
come to such as win. And, what is more, rise in the

service should also depend on a suitable test. And
here may usefully be recalled the terms of the
Queen's proclamation :—

" And it is our further will that, as far as may be,
our subjects, of whatever race or creed, be freely
and impartially admitted to offices in our service, the
duties of which they may be qualified by their education, ability, and integrity duly to discharge."

Under such a régime it might be possible in time
to see the Judicial Bench of the West African
Dependencies filled by Jurists not necessarily British
by birth. We do badly require efficiency in every
branch of the service, and we may reasonably look
for it in the administration of justice also. Men's
lives and liberties and property are matters of daily
inquiry. Inexperience may do a deal of harm;
ignorance more so. In the Universities and in the
Inns of Court there are Chairs for Mahomedan and
Roman Dutch Law, and candidates for seats on the
Magisterial Bench in South Africa or India must
satisfy a given test. There is a time coming when
a knowledge, by competitive examination, will be
required of a candidate who aspires to administer
justice either on the Gold Coast, or in Southern
Nigeria. If the place of West Africa has been
correctly indicated, it stands to reason that ancient
seats of learning will soon find it their duty to institute professorships in the Customary Laws of West
Africa. See what a mass of information would thus
be available for the solution of a given problem.
Departmental Committees would then be at a dis-
count. For there would be no necessity for the
hurried and haphazard collection of evidence on an
emergency in the face of existent scientific data and
record.

3.

The future demands also the highest possible efficiency in the West African Medical Service. We want the best brains in this Department that the Empire can produce. We aim at the excellence of the Indian Medical Service on the basis of Lord Morley's policy. Though the gradual elimination of the European doctor, either in India or in the Gold Coast, may be, for the moment, somewhat remote, it ought to be possible to give every possible encouragement to native medical men to devote their lives to scientific research in the interests of the people. The present policy of shutting the door of opportunity in the face of highly qualified native medical men is nothing short of a scandal; and one cannot but admire the manly stand that has been taken against it by the Rev. John H. Harris, of the London Aborigines Society, and others.

And there is reason for the demand. For the West African Medical Service wields a power before which the authority of Governors-General pales into insignificance. The word of its Ministers is infallible. " Their decrees, like the laws of the Medes and Persians, do not alter. When issued, Governors-General quake in their seats; policies are unsettled; commerce and enterprise stand aghast; and as for the man in the street he carries his liberty, the most sacred thing to a British subject, in his hands." Therefore it is that we must have efficiency—an efficiency which shall be gauged not by prestige, or prejudice, or favour, or the colour of a man's skin, but by the fair test of competitive examinations.

When scientific men disagree, the man in the street benefits. It leads to investigation. Scientific investigation leads to the discovery of new truths. At all events, we want to know the truth about the ways

of Stegomyia and the manner of its visitations to
the West African Dependencies. To the ordinary
man this is important. For long has he suffered
from the domination of Medical Boards. To medical
men themselves it ought to be important. For it
will remove the stigma which naturally attaches to a
divided house. It should help to restore public confidence.

In the year 1911 Sekondi was thrown into a tumult
of despair. It was proclaimed as an infected port.
Yellow fever was said to have broken out. The
pity of it was the man in the street did not believe in
it, and said so bluntly. He seemed to have had
reason on his side. For it is an historical fact that
cases that were treated outside the Colonial hospital
as for malaria recovered, whereas the cases diagnosed
by the experts as yellow fever and treated as such
succumbed. There is no harm in calling bilious remittent fever yellow fever. What's in a name? But
that there is a life to pay for every case thus wrongly
named and treated. When medical men disagree
the man in the street may have a look in. He may
even begin to use his instinct. He may be excused
if he calls in reason to his aid. And a very good
reason for suggesting a thorough investigation is
the frequency of the recurrence of these alleged outbreaks. Let us see what a well-informed writer in
the *Gold Coast Leader* in its issue of April 5, 1913,
says upon the matter :—

" Dr. Rice, Senior Sanitary Officer, in an article which
" we reproduced from the ' African Mail ' in our issue of the
" 15th March, tried to explain the reasons for recent
" epidemics or so-called epidemics of yellow fever in the
" Colony being so limited and not approaching in character
" the historical epidemics of the West Indies and South
" America. In Dr. Rice's opinion these epidemics are
" limited in the Colony because ' cases are diagnosed
" promptly, preventive measures, such as evacuation of

" the infected area and isolation of contacts, are at once put
" into force, and the campaign against the stegomyia mos-
" quito has done much to reduce the number of the defini-
" tive host; and that the promptitude with which the various
" outbreaks of 1911 were suppressed was in a large measure
" due to them.' It is, of course, satisfactory to Dr. Rice,
" who is responsible for the sanitary management of the
" Colony, and any preventive measures taken to control
" or stamp out any epidemic diseases threatening the
" Colony, to proclaim, like the good merchant, the fine
" qualities and excellence of his own wares. We would
" certainly have been among the first to give Dr. Rice the
" meed of praise he solicits, and recommend him for honours
" he may so long have desired, had we been satisfied that all
" the cases which he and his assistants diagnosed as yellow
" fever were cases of yellow fever at all.

" The Government medical officers reserve the right to
" themselves to diagnose any cases they chose as yellow
" fever cases, and nobody is to question the correctness of
" their diagnosis. The Government medical officers allow
" no consultative body or committee, consisting of them-
" selves and native private practitioners, to see, discuss,
" and form an opinion on the cases diagnosed by medical
" officers as cases of yellow fever; and in a country like this,
" where fevers of all kinds are so common, it can be per-
" ceived how easily Government medical officers, keen on
" yellow fever, can make a mistake in the diagnosis of, say,
" febricula, call that disease yellow fever, subject the Colony
" to quarantine, the people to the discomforts and hardships
" of isolation camps, outrage their feelings by unnecessary
" post-mortem examinations on their beloved dead,
" and afterwards appeal to the world to congratulate
" them on their efficiency for having stamped out
" an epidemic in quick time, and saved the
" Colony from incalculable miseries. Our readers will
" appreciate the undue advantages of the position taken up
" by the Government medical officers when we inform them
" that Sir Patrick Manson, one of the greatest authorities in
" the British Empire on tropical diseases, says that ' the
" difficulties of diagnosis of yellow fever are very great.
" There is no clinical feature so far as is known which would
" distinguish a mild attack of yellow fever from an ordinary
" febricula, nor any pathognomic clinical sign that would
" absolutely distinguish a malarial remittent from yellow
" fever.'

" It is not our desire to hamper in any way genuine work
" being done to protect or free the Colony from any epidemic
" diseases.   But we are profoundly dissatisfied with the
" methods of the present medical and sanitary advisers of
" the Government.   There seems to be a lack of the scien-
" tific spirit among the Government medical officers.   They
" appear to us to be imbued with too much class and colour
" prejudice, and their methods inspire the public with no
" confidence in the sincerity of their purpose and the single-
" ness of their aim.   They appear to us under the cloak of
" public interest to be working for their own hands and their
" own advantage."

Who can be silent in the face of such a situation?
" As far as the Gold Coast is concerned we have
had this sort of vague domination off and on for the
past two years.   The sinister flag goes up when men
think themselves most secure.   It is all done in the
name of Science.   It is high time Science decided
once and for all.   To Cæsar the servants of
Stegomyia, as far as recent outbreaks are concerned,
have appealed.   To Cæsar we will go, and it will be a
fair, open, impartial investigation in the common
forum of the scientific world."

Once more, with an efficient medical service, the
problem of population might be safely handled.   We
are not satisfied with the returns as far as the Gold
Coast is concerned.   The fairest Utopia without
children would be but a barren waste.   The causes
of infant mortality must be scientifically studied and
prevented.   We should like to see villages teeming
with chubby little ones, who would in due course
plough the field; or wield the pen, mightier than the
sword; or paint masterpieces that will astound the
world.   We want healthy children very badly in
West Africa, with its wear and tear, and that notwithstanding the prejudices of missionaries and
philanthropists.

4.

But the acme of ineffectiveness is reached when we come to that glorified Department known as the Public Works Department. How is it that in all British West Africa we cannot boast of a decent harbour, perhaps with the sole exception of the Freetown harbour? And it is on the Gold Coast that we suffer most deeply. Take that eyesore, the Accra breakwater. It is a grievous fault. It is a wanton piece of mechanism which has broken heavily into the pockets of the taxpayers, and nothing more. Everyone, official and layman alike, points at it the finger of scorn. Someone made the mistake of taking the wrong angle. The Crown Colony system is the embodiment of irresponsibility, or it would be possible to discover that somebody and make it ever afterwards impossible that a similar mistake should occur.

What of your waterworks, which take decades to finish, while the people groan with thirst? What of public buildings raised only to be condemned as unfit for habitation? For a change, it might be suggested that here, also, competition be invited. What really should it matter to this Dependency whether a French or a German firm gives us a decent, useful harbour, or whether suggestions come from the brain of an African? It has been ironically said that about the only straight line cut in the Sekondi-Coomassie line was the work of a black engineer. One may here take the opportunity of reminding the Government that there are competent native engineers on the Gold Coast—men whose parents have spent fortunes in qualifying in the different branches of the profession. But they are, generally speaking, among the unemployed. And yet these men would take a pride in the erection of useful permanent works in their own country. With the present enlightened Administration, it ought to be possible to call in the services of these men to aid the Department.

5.

And what shall we say next? The future of West Africa demands that the voice of the taxpayers should be more and more heard in the councils of West Africa. You cannot admit the place of West Africa within the Empire without admitting this fact. The Power which controls the destinies of peoples and nations calls upon us to recognise this fact. West Africa shall not for ever remain a hewer of wood and drawer of water. She shall take her true place among the nations of the earth. View her history impartially. Where can man record such astounding developments and such progress? The brain of her people is as fertile as her soil. Where, elsewhere, you have to prepare glass houses and regulated temperatures in order to produce given results, here you have only to scratch the ground, put in the seed, and presto! such results as may satisfy the most fastidious. And she shall move on to her preordained destiny, and no power on earth can stay her course. Only West Africa must believe in herself. She must realise the extent of her opportunity, and, bending her full force to the task, she must rise superior to every obstacle.

Well, it is obvious that West Africa cannot continue for ever watering the feet of the Empire without her own feet being watered. It would be against the law of Nature. You cannot be a blessing to others without you yourself being blessed. That does not depend upon the will of man. And the first substantial reward will be the enjoyment of free institutions. We do not necessarily require Parliaments after the type of that in the heart of the Empire; but some substantial sort of effective control must we have in the passing of laws and in expenditure. Then will all the vagaries that are exposed from year to year in the annals of West Africa be put a stop to.

I have in another work indicated that the claim for representative Government on the part of a West African Dependency is not based on imitation of what has been learnt from others. The idea is indigenous; so, at the least, with the Gold Coast. That this matter may also be free from controversy, I shall quote from what I have said herein before. For, on the authority of the late revered Dr. Edward Wilmot Blyden, the task of West African writers, situated as they are, must be line upon line, precept upon precept, here a little and there a little, if so be the voice that cries in the wilderness may be heard of men.

Well, ten years ago I wrote in " Gold Coast Native Institutions " thus :—

" Legislation, to be effectual, must be with the Chiefs in
" a representative legislative assembly. Any important
" measure affecting the people must be passed with ' the
" consent and the direct co-operation of the Chiefs them-
" selves.' If the policy of the Government had been based
" upon this sound principle, there would be no need to-day
" for this work. What the country requires most urgently
" to-day is a national assembly wherein all sections of the
" community will be adequately represented. That is the
" fundamental element of progress—the reform at which all
" right-thinking men must directly aim."

And this important principle is supported by Lord Stanley, Secretary of State to the Colonies, in his letter to Lieutenant-Governor Hill, on the " Assessor's Jurisdiction," dated at Downing Street, Novem-

ber 22nd, 1844, which is worth again reproducing
in this connection :—

" You will bear in mind that the power of the assessor in
" his judicial capacity is not derived from either the Acts of
" Parliament above referred to or from the Order in Council.
" . . . It must be founded on the assent and concurrence
" of the sovereign power of the State within which it is
" exercised, either expressed, as in the case of the treaty
" transmitted by you in your private and confidential
" despatch of the 6th of March last, or implied from long
" usage, as in the case of the long and general acquiescence,
" which can be shown in many districts, in the authority
" hitherto exercised by Mr. Maclean."

Again, what I said a decade ago in considering the
" Conflict of Systems " applies with yet greater force
to-day.   It was this :—

" We have seen from the discussion of native institutions
" how widely diffused among the people is the idea of repre-
" sentative government.   It is the very essence of the
" Native State system.   In that system, the right of every
" adult member of the community to be represented in the
" State Councils is fully recognised and guaranteed.   What
" conflict of ideas must there be in the mind of the native
" when he contemplates the farcical pretext in respect of
" the representation of the country in the presence of
" the non-official members of Council in the Council
" Chamber!

" The trend of progress the whole world over is toward
" free institutions—a state of society whose members are
" free to govern and regulate their own affairs.   It is the
" keynote of healthy Imperialism.   It is this very principle,
" recognised by Great Britain in her relations with the
" Dominions over the seas, which is strengthening and con-
" solidating Greater Britain.   But I shall possibly be met
" with the criticism that self-government is reserved by
" Great Britain for those English-speaking Colonies whose
" populations are nearly or wholly white.   That may be.
" But what is the essence of the matter?   I am inclined to
" think that it is not so much a question of the particular
" people inhabiting a particular Dependency, as a yielding
" to the logic of facts in given circumstances.   Statesmen,
" in time, have come to learn the hidden meaning of the

" bitter lesson which cost Great Britain the loss of the
" American Colonies, and the world one of the greatest
" opportunities of conserving universal peace, progress, and
" goodwill among men. In the case of the Gold Coast we
" shall appeal to the logic of facts, and shall not appeal in
" vain.

" I believe, therefore, that whenever a strong case has
" been made, showing the capability and the right of any
" given community in free alliance and friendship with Great
" Britain, call such connection by what name soever you
" please, to manage its own internal affairs, Great Britain
" will not be backward in extending to such a community the
" blessing of free institutions, feeling certain that therein
" lies the fastest bond with the Mother Country. In the
" case of the Gold Coast, we simply say, ' Allow us to make
" use of our own native institutions, which we understand,
" and which from experience are adapted to us.' We shall
" ask once, twice, and ask again, and if this generation is
" not listened to, we shall hand on the legacy of legitimate
" and constitutional request to the next generation.

" But where are your facts, you will rightly ask, making it
" logically proper to ask for the revival of representative
" government, on native lines, on the Gold Coast? To a
" fair question allow me to return a fair answer. I have
" endeavoured to show that, on the Gold Coast, you are not
" dealing with a savage people without a past, who are
" merely striving to copy or imitate foreign institutions. I
" can understand why, for example, you will rightly or
" wrongly refuse full representative government, say, to
" Jamaica or Trinidad. There you are not dealing with an
" indigenous people. You are face to face with the problem
" of trying to train up a people who have lost touch with
" their past, and whose immediate past dates from the
" time when Europe went into sackcloth and ashes over her
" grievous sin against the African race. You may seriously
" or not assume that they are not ripe for self-government,
" and postpone the time till the Greek calends. But here
" you are confronted with no such difficulty. On the con-
" trary, you are stimulated by the circumstances of the case.
" If you are free to admit it, you will see that you find here
" already a sysem of self-government as perfect and efficient
" as the most forward nations of the earth to-day can pos-
" sibly conceive. A people who could, indigenously, and
" without a literature, evolve the orderly representative

" government which obtained in Ashanti and the Gold
" Coast before the advent of the foreign interloper, are a
" people to be respected and shown consideration when they
" proceed to discuss questions of self-government.

" Nor in discussing this matter must we lose sight of the
" fact that the position of the Gold Coast is perfectly unique
" among all the other so-called Dependencies of Great
" Britain. Without anticipating the discussion in the next
" chapter, I may broadly state that the relations between
" Great Britain and the Gold Coast originated in friendship,
" mutual trust, and commercial alliance. It will be seen,
" therefore, that the people have a right to mould their
" institutions upon their lines, Great Britain being merely a
" protecting Power, and only concerned with their relations
" with the outside world. It will be also seen that at no
" time have the people divested themselves of their right
" to legislate for themselves. Before the spread of educa-
" tion in the land, they did these things for themselves,
" sometimes in co-operation with their friends and protec-
" tors. Why not now?

" It is sad to reflect in this connection that the policy of
" the British Government has been retrogressive rather than
" progressive. It is as if the Colonial Office had resolutely
" set to work to discourage national spirit, and to destroy
" every vestige of it in the breasts of the people. But this
" kind of thing will not do. Hence the humble appeal
" to-day that Great Britain should fully and seriously con-
" sider this question of free institutions for the Gold Coast,
" upon which so much of the future progress of the country
" depends.

" It is conceded, I believe, on all sides that the Crown
" Colony system of administering the affairs of the Gold
" Coast has failed, hopelessly failed. What then? Is the
" country to be left to go to rack and ruin? It may mean
" nothing to the colonists, but to the aborigines it means
" everything that is dear to them of country, home, and
" fatherland.

" If the Gold Coast were a country with free institutions,
" free from the trammels of Downing Street red-tapeism,
" we should soon have good wharves and harbours, gas
" works, waterworks, and railway communication all over
" the country. Prosperous cities would grow up, and know-
" ledge would spread among all classes of the people, pro-
" ducing a willing and an efficient body of workmen for the

" material development of the vast wealth and resources
" of the country.

" In a well-regulated system the whites would find they
" could not do without the blacks, and vice versa, and soon
" would grow up a spirit of forbearance, tolerance, and
" mutual respect, each race doing its allotted work upon
" natural lines in a prosperous and contented Federal Gold
" Coast and Ashanti.

" All this may be a dream. At least, so you may think.
" But if a dream, it is one worth attempting to realise,
" instead of sitting bound hand and foot in the face of ugly
" facts."

6.

I end as I began. I bring West Africa this day a
message of hope. I bring her also a message of
goodwill and high endeavour. I bid her join hands
across the sea over her common need, her common
trouble, her common anxiety, her all-important aim.
I would ask her men of light and leading to smoke
the peace-pipe together. It is a sacrament to be received with an humble heart. And united West
Africa arises chastened and inspired with the convic-
tion that in union is her strength, her weakness in
discord.

APPENDICES.

APPENDIX A.

THE BLACK MAN'S LAND.
THE OLD AND THE NEW POLICY.

A REVIEW OF SIR WILLIAM NEVIL McGEARY'S
ARTICLE IN " THE NATIONAL REVIEW,"
JANUARY, 1913.

A remarkable sermon was preached in London on Sunday evening, February 17, 1907, by the Rev. Charles Garnett, M.A. It was a manly statement on behalf of certain South African native Chiefs who needed badly an appeal as to their lands. These men, who at one time owned certain portions of the lands of South Africa, were now practically homeless, and they had come all the way to England to see if they could get a holding on African soil—fancy that —on soil which once was indisputably theirs. There were British men of honour and of high principle ready to plead the cause of the helpless, and the Rev. Charles Garnett but represented an influential section of enlightened British public opinion. And this thing is of happy augury for the future of the British Empire. When last I was in England I had the opportunity of visiting the House of Commons, the Bank of England, and other national institutions. But it was not until I found myself at the Wesleyan Conference, one of the finest deliberative bodies in the world, that I got an idea as to the staying power of England. Paradoxical, is it not? Yet men will come in time to recognise that that which makes for the highest prestige of a nation is a developed sense of fair-play, justice, and equity. Believe me, nothing impresses the African mind better than these qualities. The average African will go the wide world with you, if he can but trust you. When journals like *The Review of Reviews*, *The National Review*, and others, take to arousing the public conscience as to the rights of a defenceless people, and there are such fearless men as the writer of the article now under review to espouse their cause, one may reasonably hope that the future is not so dark.

The writer of this article, as has been noted elsewhere, was for eighteen years in the West African Colonial Civil Service, and was at one time the Attorney-General of the Gold Coast. As such he has had unique opportunities of comparing the alternative policies advocated, and, therefore, must command attention.

The writer opens this important contribution to the land question by directing attention to the two alternative land policies in West Africa, " the Northern Nigerian, and what may be generally described as the Gold Coast, Land Policy," and, continuing, informs us that it is now proposed to introduce the Northern Nigerian system throughout all the West African Colonies in substitution for the latter.

Before proceeding with the further discussion of the article, it may be useful to recall what the Right Honourable the Secretary of State to the Colonies is reported to have said upon the matter from his place in Parliament on June 27, 1912, to the effect that however excellent a land system might be, regard must be had to the circumstances of the particular Dependency where such a system is sought to be applied.

Bearing this in mind, it is easy to follow the writer when he draws attention to the importance of West Africa, and invites us to an examination of the land system of the Gold Coast in the following pregnant paragraphs :—

" In British West Africa there are twenty million " natives inhabiting about half a million square miles. " The exports are about ten million sterling; which re- " present the produce of the land, mineral, agricultural, " and natural.

" British West Africa comprises five Colonies: Gambia, " Sierra Leone, Gold Coast, Southern Nigeria and " Northern Nigeria. Northern Nigeria came under the " Crown by transfer from the Niger Company in 1900. " The other four Colonies have been British for a long " time; the Gambia and Gold Coast for two hundred " years; Lagos, the capital of Southern Nigeria, became " British in 1861. But the period of the commercial and " political rise of the four Colonies really dates from Mr. " Chamberlain's assumption of the Colonial Office. He " was a good friend to West Africa; men and money " were freely, wisely and successfully employed in what " this statesman described as the development of Unim- " proved Estates. The Gold Coast system was introduced " in 1900 on Mr. Chamberlain's instructions, and it has, " in the main, worked well and given satisfaction to Euro- " peans and natives, and there is no demand for its " reversal.

" The other four Colonies have each separate legisla- " tures and different laws. But the Land Laws are simi- " lar. Putting aside the Gambia, Sierra Leone, and " Southern Nigeria, let us examine the land system and " legislation of the Gold Coast, which may be taken as in " every way representative. The Gold Coast is not only " the oldest of the British Colonies in West Africa, but " it is therein that during the last two or three decades " European enterprise in mining and other concessions " first began and has been most widely developed. On " the Gold Coast Colony, moreover, we have the benefits " of the Belfield report, published July, 1912 (Cd. " 6278)."

The writer points out that twenty years ago there was no legislative control of alienation in West Africa.

Then was introduced the Crown Lands Bill, and, later, the Lands Ordinance, both of which measures proposed legislative experiments similar to those advocated for Northern Nigeria.

In Sir William M. Geary's own words :—

" The first legislative solutions proposed in 1894 and
" 1897 were similar to the Northern Nigerian system,
" viz., that land should be vested in or administered by
" the Government. To this the natives vigorously
" objected as being confiscation of their land. They sent
" a deputation to Mr. Chamberlain, who admitted their
" objections were well founded, and withdrew the pro-
" posed legislation. In lieu thereof the Concessions
" Ordinance, 1900, still in force, was passed on his instruc-
" tions. Mr. Chamberlain was ' master in his own
' house,' and could control Governors and permanent
" officials. Under the Concessions Ordinance the pros-
" pective European concessionary has to approach the
" chief and make his bargain with him, which teaches
" both that the latter is the owner of the land. Next the
" matter goes before the Concessions Court, to inquire
" whether they understand, whether terms are reason-
" able, and customary rights of people protected. Then
" there is a survey and, if no opposition, certificate of
" validity is issued, whereby the concessionary gets a title
" *in rem* good against all the world. The payment, which
" consists of a sum down, usually about £250, an occupa-
" tion rent about £30, and after mining commences a full
" rent about £300, is made to the Government, **who pays
" over the whole to the chief;** he keeps a third for him-
" self, a third for the " Stool," and a third he gives to the
" elders. Agricultural concessions are subject to the
" sanction of the Executive, but under similar conditions,
" the natives being the grantors and payees; the
" Governor's sanction being endorsed on the deed."

" In January, 1912, Mr. H. C. Belfield, C.M.G., an ex-
" perienced official, was sent out as Special Commissioner
" to inquire into the twelve years' working of this system.
" He stayed over two months, took the evidence of forty-
" four witnesses, a judge, officials, mining managers, the
" European lawyer representing most of the mining com-
" panies, five native lawyers, and several native chiefs,

" and also educated natives. His report was published
" about July 12. Mr. Belfield finds as facts:—

" 1. That while the Crown extends its protective
" authority to all places and persons in the Colony, there
" is vested in it no right of ownership in any lands save
" the forts on the coast, with the adjacent area and land
" specially acquired, and any endeavour to extend these
" rights otherwise than by the legal process of acquisi-
" tion would amount to a breach of faith with the people.

" 2. That all the land belongs to the people. The land
" is divided among tribes with boundaries which, though
" approximate, are known. The tenure of this land is
" communal, with the exception of individual land
" usually near the coast town. The land not required for
" tribal use is vested in the chiefs and elders, and the
" proceeds applied as above explained; misconduct and
" misappropriation being punished by removal from office.
" Mr. Belfield, in his recommendations approves of the
" principle of the chief and elders being the grantors and
" payees of concessions to Europeans, subject to official
" intervention.

" But such intervention must be conducted in a man-
" ner which will leave the people assured that their in-
" herent right of disposition of their lands remains in their
" own hands, and that only such interference is contem-
" plated as will supplement their knowledge of essential
" detail, and obviate the risk of their knowingly making
" bad bargains, while leaving to themselves the right of
" election as to whether the land applied for shall be
" disposed of or withheld. On no account must the fact
" be lost sight of that the land is the property of the
" people, that a concession is a contract between the land-
" owners and the applicant to which the Government is
" no party; that intervention must therefore be limited
" to supervision and guidance only, to the end that im-
" provident alienation may be prevented and only such
" terms sanctioned as will ensure adequate protection of
" the rights and requirements of present and future gene-
" rations.

" Such a land system appears to combine the minimum
" of interference by the State with the maximum of pro-
" tection for the subject. One quarter of the premium
" and rent, he recommends to be retained by the Govern-
" ment, to be expended locally on works of permanent

" public utility. He recommends the abolition of the
" Concessions Court, and that each kind of concession
" should be passed by the Executive. This might be
" theoretically better, but the native has a great liking for
" being heard in Court, and will always prefer the deci-
" sion of a Law Court exalted above the arena of the
" administrative conflict to the decision of the most fair
" and honest official. He testifies to the bona fides both
" in representative constitution of membership and finan-
" cial status of the Gold Coast Aborigines' Protection
" Society, consisting of chiefs and educated native traders
" and lawyers. This is the Society which has criticised in
" the past Government Bills and is opposing the present
" proposals."

The Concessions Ordinance practically controls
alienation wherein foreign capitalists are the grantees
of concessions, and the writer takes care to point out
that " Native land tenure and dealing between native
and native is left to Native Common Law and there is
no legislation thereon in any of the four colonies."

We next get an illuminating contrast between the
Gold Coast land system and that of Northern Nigeria.
He tells us that :—

· " In Northern Nigeria the law is entirely different. The
" surface owner has no benefit from the mine. In 1902
" Sir Frederick Lugard declared to the Sultan of Sokoto:
" ' The Government will have the right to all minerals,
" but the people may dig for iron and work it, subject to
" the approval of the High Commissioner, and may take
" salt and other minerals, subject to any exercise imposed
" by law.'* Legislation followed on these lines, so that
" in Northern Nigeria the surface owner derives neither
" dead rent nor royalty from the European-owned mine.
" One does not see on what basis of right this vesting
" of all mines in the Government can be justified. It is
" not the law of England, whereby mines belong to the
" surface owner except mines of gold and silver which
" belong to the Crown. Probably the reason why this
" Crown prerogative was allowed to subsist after the

---

* Blue Book, N. Nigeria, Report 1904 (Cd. 1768), pp. 58 & 153.

" abolition of 1660 of the feudal tenures, is that gold and
" silver mines in England are as unimportant as the pre-
" rogative rights to whales and sturgeon. The tin mines
" of Northern Nigeria, according to evidence before the
" Commission of 1908, were worked by the natives pre-
" vious to the coming of the European companies, who
" sometimes, at all events, expelled the native worker.
" Generally in all European concessions—mines or other—
" the native of Northern Nigeria has neither voice
" as to the grant, nor benefit from the workings ;
" the application is to Government, who receive the rent ;
" any natives actually on the land are, however, entitled
" to compensation."

" Apart from European concessions, the Land Pro-
" clamation of 1910, has regulated native land tenure
" throughout Northern Nigeria. It has been enacted
" that all land occupied or unoccupied (except the Niger
" Company's land) is to be ' native land,' under the con-
" trol and disposition of the Governor, and no title to
" occupation or use is to be valid without the consent of
" the Governor. The Governor is enabled to give a cer-
" tificate of right of occupancy at a rental to be revised
" every seven years. Such right of occupancy devolves
" upon death according to native custom. But the occu-
" pier has no right of alienation, *inter vivos,* either by
" sale, mortgage, or transfer of possession, without the
" previous consent of the Governor, and any such
" attempted alienation is null and causes a forfeiture of
" the right of occupancy. As regards involuntary aliena-
" tion by execution or bankruptcy the Proclamation is
" silent. This legislation applies not only to farms, but
" to houses in urban sites. This legislation was the result
" of the Report of the Committee of 1908."*

The article now proceeds to deal frankly with the
composition of the Committee. It says plainly :—

" But it is open to criticise the constitution and pro-
" ceedings of the Committee. The report involves the
" absolute denial of the natives' property in the land he
" occupies, and it is the report of a Committee who were
" in a hurry—their instructions were to hurry ; they took
" evidence in six days and finished in two months. All

---

* 1910 (Cd. 5102, 3).

" the members of the Committee were officials or ex-
" officials, with the exception of Mr. J. Wedgwood, M.P.
" The character and good intentions of these gentlemen is
" unimpeachable and unimpeached. But when the
" issue to be tried is as to the ownership of land between
" the Government and the natives, can it be satisfactory
" to the latter that the majority of the tribunal should be
" employés or ex-employés of the former, especially when
" their verdict is in favour of the former and the latter
" has no opportunity of being heard either in person or by
" counsel?

" With one exception, Mr. J. Holt, all the witnesses
" were officials or ex-officials. Besides J. Holt and Co.,
" the only other European traders in Northern Nigeria
" were the Niger Company. They declined to give evi-
" dence on the ground that the subject being of great mag-
" nitude it was impossible to consider it in the few days
" given. The Committee began its sittings on June 1,
" 1908; the Niger Company were only invited to give
" evidence on July 10, and the Committee closed its evi-
" dence on July 17, and reported on July 29, 1908.

" Another important omission was that no native was
" admitted to give evidence. No evidence was admitted
" to show how the Gold Coast Concessions Ordinance had
" worked though witnesses thereon were available in
" England as well as in Africa. No missionary gave evi-
" dence—and a missionary may be a most important wit-
" ness; for, like a trader, he knows the native and his
" ways and customs from an unofficial standpoint, and he
" is independent of the Government in a way no official,
" and few trading agents, can be. Roman Catholic Mis-
" sionaries' evidence would have been valuable, as in
" three cases they were vendors of land to the Niger Com-
" pany, and they might have been asked from whom and
" how they acquired the land."

As to the value of the Committee's finding we have
the following criticism :—

" The Committee reported that the native has no ' pro-
" perty ' in the land he occupies. But I think I have
" shown that their decision must be accepted with some
" reserve. Even taking the evidence given, there is room
" for a different conclusion, viz., that the occupying cul-
" tivator had by custom undisturbed possession subject to

" some fine on alienation. Nor do I think it lies in the
" mouth of the British Government to deny the natives'
" rights of property and alienation. The Niger Company,
" from 1880 to 1900, bought from the natives various
" rights over land, freehold, leasehold, and easements, and
" in 1900 part of these rights they sold to the Govern-
" ment and part retained. If the natives had no right
" to alienate to the Niger Company, then the British
" Government have no title to these lands."

" Further, as the British Government bought in 1900
" from the Niger Company land and rights over land
" which the Niger Company had originally acquired from
" natives, why should land now occupied by natives be
" taken and vested in the British Government by mere
" act of law. The assertion of ' control ' by the Govern-
" ment under the Proclamation of 1910 is not technical, as
" they are enabled to take actual possession of any land,
" if required, without payment for the land, but only for
" crops and improvements."

After this the writer turns to the " present situation " and discusses most ably Mr. Belfield's report.
Says he :—

" Lastly, let us turn to the present situation.   Mr.
" Belfield's report was published on or about July 12, 1912,
" but this official gentleman returned to England on May
" 14, 1912, and naturally he must have at once called at
" the Colonial Office ; presumably he informed them of the
" general purport of his report, but to the Colonial Office
" only must it have been known.   On June 6, 1912, there
" appeared in the 'Times ' a letter signed by E. D. Morel,
" Noel Buxton, J. Ramsay Macdonald, Philip Morell,
" Albert Spicer, and Josiah C. Wedgwood, urging that the
" Northern Nigerian land system should be applied
" throughout West African Colonies, and that an experi-
" enced Committee should be appointed, as was done in
" the case of Northern Nigeria.   On the same June 6,
" 1912, a deputation, including E. D. Morel, Mr. Wedg-
" wood, P. Morell, Mr. N. Buxton, and Mr. King, waited
" on Mr. L. Harcourt at the Colonial Office to urge that
" the Northern Nigeria system should be applied to the
" other West African Colonies.   In the ' Times ' of June
" 26, 1912, there is an announcement that the Secretary
" of State for the Colonies has appointed a Committee ' to

" consider the laws relating to the transfer of land in the
" West African Colonies and Protectorates (other than
" Northern Nigeria), and to report whether any, and if so
" what, amendments of the law is required.' The per-
" sonnel of the Commission are Sir Kenelm E. Digby,
" G.C.B., K.C., Chairman; Sir F. M. Hodgson,
" K.C.M.G., Sir W. Taylor, K.C.M.G., Mr. J. C. Wedg-
" wood, Mr. E. D. Morel, with Mr. C. Strachey, Mr. W.
" D. Ellis, and Mr. R. E. Stubbs, of the Colonial Office.
" Out of these eight gentlemen three—Sir K. E. Digby,
" Mr. J. C. Wedgwood, and Mr. C. Strachey, were mem-
" bers of the Northern Nigerian system and took part in
" the deputation. The remaining four members of the
" Committee are officials or ex-officials.

" The inference seems obvious that the Colonial Office,
" who alone knew the purport of the Belfield Report, pub-
" lished July 12, 1912, were not the *Agent Provocateur*
" of the letter and deputation of June 6, 1912, but also by
" the appointment on June 26 of the Committee above
" named, were determined to effect the throwing over of
" the Belfield Report and the introduction throughout
" West Africa of the Northern Nigerian system. Some,
" if not the majority, of the Committee, had already pre-
" judged the question submitted to them, and announced
" their preference for the Northern Nigerian system."

As to the composition of the Committee, the Liver-
pool Chamber of Commerce decided at its meeting of
July 1st, 1912, " to support a strong protest by the
African Trade Section against the composition of a
Committee appointed by the Secretary of State for the
Colonies to consider land transfer in West Africa,
which, said Mr. G. A. Moore, had been too long the
sport of faddists."

The writer next takes up the argument in favour
of West African land nationalisation and against improvident alienation of " tribal lands." Says he :—

" The arguments in favour of the Northern Nigerian
" system and its introduction elsewhere may be gathered
" from the report and evidence given before the Com-
" mittee of 1908, Mr. E. D. Morel's articles in his paper,
" the ' African Mail,' and the letter of June 6, 1912.

" They are twofold, *i.e.*, that by nationalising the land
" the introduction of freehold individual tenure, which
" has already shown a tendency to creep in is prevented,
" and alleged communal system preserved ; and secondly,
" the chiefs are stopped from improvidently alienating
" the tribal lands.

" The first argument refers to native tenure and dealings
" between natives.   It is a most difficult matter for Euro-
" pean officials to understand, codify, and administer
" native law, and unless there is an imperative necessity,
" they had much better leave it alone.   Why should not
" individual ownership come in Northern Nigeria, as it has
" come in elsewhere?   Politically, a peasant proprietor-
" ship owing security of tenure to the British Govern-
" ment seems a valuable asset.   Economically, to forbid
" by law the individual African ever becoming the owner
" of the land he occupies, removes the strongest induce-
" ment to thrift, good farming, and development of the
" country.   There are arguments in favour of land
" nationalisation and in particular of the nationalisation of
" mines, which it is not my task here to discuss.   But in
" Europe, as a matter of practical politics, such nation-
" alisation could only be carried out by compensation or
" recognition of existing vested rights, unless as the result
" of a bloody civil war or revolution.   In Northern Nigeria
" it has been effected not only without the consent but
" without consulting the natives and without any saving
" of vested interests.   The arguments, such as they are,
" in favour of land nationalisation, lose much of their
" force if it is to be thrust on the landsfolk at the behest
" and apparently for the benefit of an alien Power and its
" officials.   Imagine land nationalisation in England car-
" ried out by a German conquest and the proceeds applied
" to the garrison and administration of the conquerors.
" To allow a communal native system, with its give and
" take, to continue or die out is far different from laying
" down by statute a hard and fast Government control,
" administered by zealous officials.

" The second argument is that by improvident aliena-
" tions to Europeans of large areas and tribal land for a
" trifling consideration, the tribe will be deprived of their
" land and reduced—the phrase is Mr. Morel's—to a land-
" less native proletariat.

" Even assuming this to be either true in the present or
" a risk in the future, this is no reason for interfering with

" native land tenure and dealings between natives. But
" it is not true in the present, and with any prudent legis-
" lative control over concessions there is no risk of the
" African being excluded from the soil by *latifundia*. Here
" we can come to bed-rock facts; the Belfield Report
" finds:—

" (a) Only one twenty-seventh of the Gold Coast and
" hardly any of Ashanti has been alienated to European
" concessionaries.

" (b) There is over and above sufficient land for triple
" the present native population.

" (c) The natives welcome the introduction of Euro-
" pean concessionaires under proper conditions, and their
" presence is beneficial to the natives.

" The demand for concessions rightly granted cannot en-
" croach seriously on the supply of land for the native.
" Each of these classes of concessions must surely be
" considered in a different light as to whether they are
" or are not exclusive of native rights to cultivation, of
" gathering natural produce, of hunting, &c.

" (1) For a mining concession the exclusive surface
" required would extend to but a few acres for the shaft,
" erection of plant, houses for staff and labourers, dump-
" ing-ground, and the right to cut timber for props and
" fuel. A mining concession might therefore be granted
" over a large area with but trifling interference with
" native rights. Suppose, to put an extreme case, the
" whole half-million square miles of British West Africa
" were parcelled out among various mining companies
" subject to forfeiture for non-working or non-payment of
" rent, would there be any material interference with the
" surface rights of the natives?

" (2) A timber concession is not exclusive of native
" rights, and according to Mr. Belfield's suggestion,
" paragraphs 126 and 127, would be for five years only at a
" dead rent and royalty to remove mahogany ripe for
" cutting.

" (3) Agricultural concessions for planting rubber,
" cocoa, &c., must of course be *pro tanto* exclusive of
" native rights. But if, as Mr. Belfield suggests in para-
" graph 114 such a concession should be not more than two
" square miles in a block, and not more than two such
" areas held by the same person—it will be a very long

" time before the half-million square miles in British West
" Africa are planted up by European concessionaires. A
" grazing concession might be treated similarly to an agri-
" cultural concession, but up till now the European has
" manifested no wish to become a West African ' Cattle
" Baron.

" (4) A concession of gathering natural sylvan produce-
" oils, palms, gum, rubber, &c., should never be granted
" —see paragraphs 18 and 19 of Sir P. Girouard's des-
" patch—as a monopoly and to the exclusion of the
" natives.

" A common-sense purview of these facts as to Euro-
" pean concessions drives one to the inference that the
" argument as to improvident alienation is so baseless, it
" can only be a pretext to cover some different object,
" which the native, who is both shrewd and suspicious,
" has already perceived. The African objects, and natur-
" ally, that the control and disposition of his land should
" be vested in the Government, and that he should become
" a rent payer on a precarious tenure. If the Colonial
" Office have a cast iron policy they mean to enforce, it
" is open to them to carry it out. The natives are helpless
" and know they are helpless. At the most there will be
" some occasional village riot, whereof the victims will be
" many score black men and some luckless British subal-
" tern or sub-official. Is it the pretext to introduce the
" Indian Land Tax at 6s. in the pound, resulting in a
" population always near starvation limit? "

" Cui bono "? To what purpose is all this ado?
We will answer it in Sir William M. Geary's own
inimitable way :—

" ' Cui Bono ' is the question to be asked as to the pre-
" sent proposal looked at with regard to the interests of
" the British Government, the natives and the European
" concessionary.

" The European concessionary's interests are confined
" to dealings between natives and Europeans. He has no
" interest in dealings between natives and natives. He
" wants only a good merchantable indefeasible Govern-
" ment guaranteed title, which he can put and sell upon
" the Stock Exchange. He has to pay premiums and
" rent either to the Government or to the natives, and
" *prima facie* it would seem immaterial to him who will be

" the payee. But the interest of the European conces-
" sionary is to live peaceably with the surrounding natives
" and obtain a good and constant supply of labour. That
" the native should be the payee will contribute to both
" these ends. The African is shrewd enough to appre-
" ciate the inexpediency of eating the gold-egg laying
" goose. If he perceives that the sequence of no labour
" and no profits for the concessionary means no rent to
" native, it will surely conduce better to the peaceful
" development of the country than taxes and police.

" The native accepts generally the theory that land
" dealings between natives and Europeans should be sub-
" ject to external sanction, provided that he is the payee,
" and he prefers the sanction should be judicial rather
" than executive."

Lastly there is a pregnant postcript which the
reader cannot afford to ignore. And it is this :—

" Northern Nigeria is excluded from the purview of the
" now sitting Committee, but if the Gold Coast native dis-
" likes the Northern Nigerian system, perhaps the
" Northern Nigerian native would like the present Gold
" Coast system ; and they might, which has not yet been
" done, be consulted as to their wishes. In the Gold
" Coast system the European concessionary pays rent to
" the native ; in Northern Nigeria the native pays rent to
" the European Government."

I have allowed Sir William McGeary to speak
almost throughout in his own words, and for an
obvious reason. I have said that there are two sides to
every question. Mr. Morel and his set have elected to
see only one side of this question. That the other point
of view is logical, equitable, and supported by an
authority of Mr. Morel's own creation is evident, not
only from the representations of "educated
natives," but also from the calm survey of disinterested men capable of judging the situation. These
things being so, will the public conscience of Britain
allow an injustice to be done to the West African
peoples, or will their appeal merit the attention which
it deserves? For ourselves, we believe, West Africa
will calmly and hopefully await the decision.

APPENDIX B.

"THE CAPE COAST VISIT.

1.

THE GOVERNOR'S ARRIVAL.

Grand Reception by the Inhabitants of Cape Coast.

"The ancient town of Cape Coast wore a festive appearance on the morning of Thursday, the 15th inst., when His Excellency Sir Hugh Charles Clifford, K.C.M.G., Governor and Commander-in-Chief, accompanied by his suite, consisting of Capt. Hamilton-Dalrymple, A.D.C., Mr. Holme, private secretary, and his medical attendant Dr. C. V. Lefanu, M.B., Ch.B., &c., &c., Acting Principal Medical Officer, landed ex s.s. *Tarquah* at 8.30 a.m. Hours before His Excellency's arrival the whole town was astir, and both old and young were preparing to accord him a warm welcome. It was a gala day, and the future historian would be charged with a dereliction of duty if he failed to make the 15th of May, 1913, stand out in bold relief in chronicling the notable events of the year. Merchants and traders closed their shops throughout the day, all the schools, elementary and secondary, were vacated in honour of Sir Hugh's arrival, and everyone assisted to make the occasion auspicious and unique.

"The elaborate programme of the Cape Coast Town Reception Committee was carried out without a hitch.

The day and Sunday school children, in holiday attire, lined the streets from Castle Beach Road to Victoria Park in the following order :—The Beach through Low Town Road was occupied by the girls and boys of the Government schools and Sunday school; from the Main Drain at the junction of King Aggrey Street were the Wesleyan day and Sunday school children; the Catholic and the African Methodist Episcopal Zion Mission schools and Sunday schools were posted at Jackson Street; the Nigritian children were formed along Green Lattice Lane; the students of the S.P.G. Grammar School occupied the street abutting on the Broach and the Mfantsipim and Richmond College students took their stand along the Gothic House, thus making a long lane of human walls on the right and on the left. At the landing places things were moving forward, and such was the congested mass of people hurrying to and fro that the police had their work cut out for them. District and Provincial Kings and Chiefs in state were constantly passing with their retinue to take their positions at the Park, making melody and adding to the volume of noise the occasion demanded. Massed choristers in surplice to the number of 80 and collected from the Anglican, Wesleyan, Zion, and Nigritian Churches were posted near the gateway leading to the Beach, and under the *baton* of C. E. Graves, Esq., A.Mus., L.C.M., F.V.C.M. Punctually at 8.30 His Excellency's boat was seen making its way towards the shore. The surf was a bit rough, and all on *terra firma* watched the progress of the boat with anxiety; presently there was a calm, and the men shot their steady craft through the swollen tide, and the Governor was lifted bodily and safely conveyed to land. A special State Umbrella already unfurled was at once placed over him, and under that regal canopy His Excellency was received by the Provincial Commissioner, J. T. Furley, Esq., and the District

Commissioner, L. W. S. Long, Esq., and other
Government officials.   The C.C.P. then walked up
by the side of Sir Hugh, and coming a little nearer
the choristers sung lustily the National Anthem, after
which he was introduced to Chief Kofi Sackey the
Regent, Tufuhin Coker, and other Chiefs of Cape
Coast; the Governor next shook hands with the offic-
cials of the Town Council, ministers of the Gospel,
members of the Bar, the officers and members of the
Aborigines' Society, and a few ladies present, including Mrs. G. H. Savage and Miss Cole.   Passing
through the entrance into Castle Beach Road, where
a guard of honour had been formed by the soldiers of
the West African Frontier Force and Gold Coast
Volunteers, under the command of Captain Harrison
and Lieutenant Blackmore, His Excellency inspected
the troops.   Preceded by the Tufuhin the Governor
and a large crowd following passed through the lines
of children surrounded by a concourse of delighted
people.   The thought atmosphere was most helpful,
for once the utmost unity prevailed among all classes,
colour and creed.   All the sweet treble voices of the
young folk blended with the deep tones of oldsters
gave hearty welcome to His Excellency; handker-
chiefs waved continuously, cheers were spontaneously
given, and, the Governor saluting them the while,
marched through the serried ranks of an excited
populace.   The tense feeling of a waiting people held
in suspense for many years found full vent when the
pleasing, open countenance of the Governor beamed
upon them.   Amusement, satisfaction, and an agree-
able surprise were a few of the sensations depicted on
the Governor's face when now and again women
waved their shawls and danced with joy before him.
The gentle sex expressed their feelings and added to
the words of welcome, tender phrases and ejacula-
tory prayers such as, " Stay with us for all time ";
" Take good care of us "; " Be a father to us ";

" Free our town from all oppression "; " Make Cape
Coast prosperous," and so forth.   Meantime at
regular intervals and at certain stations the Companies in proper order were firing volleys one after
the other.   No. 2 Company blazed away at Low Town
near the flag-staff of the Lighterage Co.; at No. 5
Company Post, the No. 5 people fired; No. 3 Company did like service near the Silk Cotton tree in
front of Captain Quansah's house; facing Millers'
Factory No. 6 Company displayed their flag, as others
had done before them, and discharged their guns,
the sound of which seemed as if they had been
loaded right up to the muzzle; at King Street, facing
the road to Fort William and Swanzy's Factory, the
No. 1 Company had their turn; No. 7 Company occupied the road to Wesleyan Mission House; and at
Commissioner Road, the No. 4 Company had their
innings; and considering the heavy detonation of
the muskets used, it was a miracle that there were no
explosions.   To the credit of the Inspector of Police
and the highly efficient management of Chief Coker
be it said, that there was only one accident caused
by reckless firing, which unfortunately grazed the
chin of a pantry boy among His Excellency's
entourage.   Inside the entrance to the Park, the
members of the Wesleyan and Nigritian Singing
Bands, assisted by the girls of the Choral Union of the
Zion Church rendered " God save the King " in the
vernacular under the conduct of Captain Abokyi,
The wording of it was as follows :—

" Nyami ngye hen Hin Pa,
   Hen Hin Kunyin nnyin nkyer,
   Nyami ngye Hin !
   Omman' Kunyimdzi daa
   Ahumka na enyimnyam,
   Ma onhwe hen du nkyer,
   Nyami ngye Hin !"

"The Park was literally seething with crowds of people. It was like a Paradise reflecting the variegated hues of the rainbow. Large contingents from the country in martial array; Kings and Chiefs from the Province with thousands of followers, muskets in hand, each itching to draw the trigger and help to make confusion worse confounded. All sorts and conditions of people had foregathered to do homage to the King's Representative, and considering the heterogeneous character of the spectators, it is a matter for congratulation that everything went on as smoothly as it did. At the centre of the Park the Boy Scouts, under the command of Scoutmaster Renner formed a guard of honour, and, arriving on the scene, the Governor inspected the lines. Our Natural Rulers had been grouped in a semi-circle, and beginning from the beginning His Excellency and suite, escorted by the Provincial and the District Commissioners formally greeted the following Kings : Moussa of the Mohammedan Community; Adzikessi of Moree; Mbia of Egya; Amonoo V. of Anamaboe; Ewusi Tsinasi of Dominasi; Kaye II. of Denkerah; Ababio II. of Aburah; Bainn of Salt Pond; Essandoh III. of Nkusukum, and the King of Esikuma; the representatives of Ahinkura of Assin Atanasu; Tsibu of Assin Apimenim; Attah Fua of Akim Kotoku; the Regent and Chiefs of Cape Coast; Princes Abakuma of Ekroful Nyanfueku and the Regent of Assaybu. The Governor, proceeding on, passed through the lines of officers and members of the following Societies in gorgeous regalia and tunics, viz. :—The Independent Order of Good Templars under the respective Constitutions of England and America; the Sons of Temperance; the Orders of Free Gardeners, Foresters, and Odd Fellows. His Excellency was then led to the Grand Stand designed by Mr. J. Bessa Simons, which he had beautifully decorated; the Governor's suite and sisters Winifred Haigh and

Mabel Robinson also took their seats by permission
of His Excellency; then the principal business of the
day began in real earnest.

2.

"WELCOME ADDRESSES.

"Cape Coast,

"15th May, 1913.

"To His Excellency,
"Sir Hugh Charles Clifford, K.C.M.G.,
Governor and Commander-in-Chief, Gold Coast
Colony and Protectorate.

"Sir,

"As Officers and Members of the Executive
Committee of the Gold Coast Aborigines' Rights Protection Society, and speaking on behalf of the Amanhin and Ahinfu (Kings and Chiefs) of the Central Province, some of whom are here assembled, we respectfully beg to offer your Excellency a most cordial
welcome to our historic town of Cape Coast.

"It was with intense gratification that we received
authentic report of your decided intention to honour
us with an official visit, and we felicitate ourselves
upon having your Excellency with us to-day.

"For obvious reasons we regard your presence here
at this opportune time as a good augury for the
material prosperity of every section of the community.

"Representing as we do, Sir, the Natural Rulers of
the Eastern, Western, and Central Provinces of this

country, we are in a position to assure your Excellency of the loyalty, goodwill, and sympathy of those whom Providence has placed under your rule and governance, and we are fully prepared and ready to accord you that frank co-operation which your Excellency has seen fit to demand and without which it would be exceedingly difficult for the Government of the Colony to be successfully administered in the interest and for the welfare of the indigenes.

"Your Excellency's thoughtful visit inspires us with renewed confidence and durable hope—confidence in His Majesty's Government and hope in the future of our rich but undeveloped country.

"There are a few matters of vital importance and urgency to which we would wish to invite your Excellency's serious attention and favourable consideration during your short stay in Cape Coast.   We flatter ourselves to think that we have discovered the key to the situation, whereby rapid progress in every direction might be facilitated in this and other places both urban and rural, especially in the Central Province; and when a satisfactory solution of such problems as may be humbly brought to your Excellency's notice shall have been effected with that breadth of sympathetic interest we have already learned to associate with your name, nothing, we trust, shall prevent or retard the social, intellectual, and economic advancement of the Gold Coast Colony and Protectorate.

"Sir, we had looked forward with pleasurable anticipation to the conjoined visit of Lady Clifford, your beloved consort. It is a sore disappointment to us that for reasons of health she is not by your side on this occasion, and we fervently pray that it may soon be possible for her ladyship to return from Europe perfectly restored to take her distinguished

place among us and render to your Excellency that
unique assistance in the services of the Colony which
only a lady of her varied experience, vast resources,
conspicuous ability and brilliant attainments could
give with credit to herself and satisfaction to us all.

" In conclusion, we commend your Excellency to the
unerring guidance of the Almighty and indulge the
hope that your maiden visit to Cape Coast may be
fraught with the highest and best results to all concerned.

God Save the King.

J. P. Brown, President.

Attoh-Ahuma, Secretary.

"His Excellency the Governor, addressing the President, Officers, and members of the Gold Coast Aborigines' Rights Protection Society, regretted that circumstances were not very propitious that morning
for one who desired to be distinctly heard. He
thanked them warmly for the magnificent reception
that had been given to him on this the occasion of his
visit to their ancient town. He hoped before leaving
Cape Coast to have further and more convenient
opportunity to meet and discuss with them important
matters connected with the affairs of the Colony. He
thanked them for the kind references they had made
to his wife, and greatly regretted her ladyship's
inability to be by his side. He hoped Lady Clifford
would be able to join him before the close of his
present tour. In a letter he had received the previous day, Lady Clifford, who had peculiar and espe-
cial interest in the town of Cape Coast, had expressed
much regret that she could not be with him that day.
His Excellency, continuing, said he trusted by the
grace of God he might be guided to administer the

government of the Colony faithfully and to the best of his ability. He would always welcome advice from every section of the community, and would be prepared to discuss matters very dear to the hearts of them all.

Cape Coast, 15/5/13.

"To His Excellency,
Sir Hugh Charles Clifford, K.C.M.G., Governor and Commander-in-Chief of the Gold Coast Colony and Protectorate.

"Your Excellency,

"We, the undersigned Regent, Tufuhin, Chiefs, Elders, Captains, and other inhabitants of Cape Coast beg most respectfully to welcome your Excellency to this town.

"Our gratification at seeing your Excellency this day is deepened by the fact that for the past six years or more we have been denied the pleasure and honour of any visit by your predecessors; and we look upon this occasion as one of great promise to us, for your Excellency will personally be in touch with all that goes on around you, and be able to make up your mind as to what is really required.

"We need not for the present take more of your Excellency's time, as you are staying beyond this day; and we hope you will afford us an opportunity of placing before your Excellency our views and wants.

"We must not omit to make mention of your Excellency's consort, Lady Clifford, who we are certain would have been pleased to accompany your Excellency here had it not been for her enforced absence

on health considerations, which we sincerely deplore.
And it is our heartfelt hope and prayer that she may
soon recover, and, if possible, return to join your
Excellency on the Coast, taking her share in the
burden of administration by her wise and genial
counsel.

„ That your health will in no way be affected by
your stay here, and that great success will always
attend your Excellency's noble efforts for the
advancement of the people over whom you are
placed.

"We beg to remain, your Excellency's most humble
servants.   (Signed)

KOFI SAKYI, *Regent.*

W. Z. COKER, *Tufuhin.*

&c., &c., &c.

"The Governor stated in reply that he could not find
words sufficiently adequate to thank them for the reception that morning.   It had been remarked in one
of the previous addresses that the people of this country were loyal to His Majesty the King, and if anyone
doubted it, he should only be there to witness the cordial reception.   His Excellency had spent a great
deal of time travelling through the Provinces, in
order to have the chance of meeting the Native Rulers
of the country, so that he might hear from their own
lips something of their feelings, thoughts and wants,
and to discuss with them the affairs and needs of
their people.   By being in touch with them, he
hoped to become sufficiently equipped for the administration of that important Colony.   He looked forward to the few days he would stay in Cape Coast
with very great interest, and he hoped that that
visit would be the first of many.

" An Address of Welcome to
His Excellency Sir Hugh Clifford, Knight
Commander of the Most Distinguished Order of
Saint Michael and Saint George, Governor and
Commander-in-Chief of the Gold Coast Colony.

"Presented by the President and Members of the
Cape Coast Town Council.

"May it please your Excellency.

" We, the President and Members of the Cape Coast
Town Council beg most respectfully to accord to
your Excellency in the name and on behalf of the
Municipality a hearty welcome to this ancient town,
and to express to your Excellency our humble felicita-
tions on your appointment as Governor and Commander-in-Chief of this Colony.

" Your Excellency's visit to this town is the cause of
much gratification to all the inhabitants, and in voic-
ing this sentiment on their behalf we as a body wish
to assure your Excellency of our earnest desire to
work for the benefit and improvement of the conditions of those whom we represent.

"We may remind your Excellency that whatever
may be its present position commercially this town
was at one time the seat of the Government. It has
been and still is the centre of much educational
activity.

" We much regret the untoward circumstances of the
illness of Lady Clifford so soon after your Excellency's arrival in the Colony, which necessitated her
ladyship's premature return to England. We know

that we are echoing the sentiments of all in stating that your Excellency's anxiety during her ladyship's illness was shared by the whole community, and we join in the general prayer that you may both be vouchsafed the enjoyment of health and every blessing throughout your Excellency's tenure of office.

"Sealed with the common seal of the Cape Coast Town Council this fourteenth day of May, One Thousand Nine Hundred and Thirteen.

(Signed)

J. T. FURLEY, *President.*

J. E. SAMPSON, *Town Clerk.*

L.S.

"His Excellency thanked the Councillors, headed by the Provincial Commissioner—J. T. Furley, Esq., as President, for the kind reception that he had had on his arrival. He also thanked them for the kind reference to his wife, who had hoped to be by his side. He trusted that an opportunity would be afforded him to discuss with them matters relating to the Town Council with more leisure and under more peaceful surroundings than those by which they were environed that morning.

"The incessant and promiscuous booming of guns fired simultaneously, very much interfered with the proceedings, and it was not possible for anything that was being said to be heard outside the radius of those who stood very close to the platform. After these addresses His Excellency bade the people *Au Revoir.*

"OUR MEMORANDUM.

"Aborigines' Office,
"Cape Coast Castle
"16th May, 1913.

"To His Excellency,

"Sir Hugh Clifford, K.C.M.G., Governor and Commander-in-Chief, Gold Coast Colony.

"May it please your Excellency,

"We, the undersigned President, ex-President, Vice-Presidents, and other officers of the Gold Coast Aborigines' Rights Protection Society, for ourselves and on behalf of the Amanhin, Ahinfu (Kings and Chiefs) of the Eastern, Western, and Central Provinces of the Gold Coast, beg leave respectfully to place the following matters of vital importance before your Excellency for your Excellency's favourable consideration.

"1. The Land Question. There is no matter which is nearer the hearts of the people of this country than the Land Question. In so far as this matter is affected by the Forest Bill and the proposed control and administration of the land by the Government, the matter has been already dealt with by our deputation to the Colonial Secretary, at the Colonial Office, London, and we desire on the present occasion to endorse all that our deputation have said and done in our behalf. In brief, the people strongly object to their lands passing under Government control and to the extension to this country in any shape or form, of the Northern Nigeria land policy.

"2. Railway Communication. We desire to call your Excellency's attention to the extreme importance of a line of railway being constructed from Cape Coast to Prahsu and another line from Cape

Coast through Jukwa and Mampon to Imbraim to tap the produce centres. This, in our humble opinion, is the key to the progress and development of the Central Province, which is the only Province, at present, without any transport facilities.

" 3. Harbour Works. Under this head, your Excellency, the construction of a breakwater at Cape Coast would appear to be a desideratum. This matter was, some years ago, brought to the notice of the Government, and an estimate therefor provided, but, up to the present, nothing has been done, and landing at Cape Coast is still dangerous.

"4. Revenue. In this connection, we would respectfully call your Excellency's attention to the necessity for a policy of retrenchment to be introduced, whereby the constant depletion of the revenue by the short service system in vogue and the "duty " and various other allowances might be guarded against. We understand that these extra allowances were introduced during the mining boom to prevent officials leaving the service for mining speculations.

" 5. Non-continuity of Policy. Another important matter to which we respectfully desire to draw your Excellency's attention is, that where a community has found an officer of the Government efficient, practical, and sympathetic, they might be permitted to ask for his return after his furlough, so as to ensure a continuity of policy.

"6. Multiplicity of Offices. We also beg to be permitted to mention the creation of certain offices which appear to us to be superfluous. For example —the appointment of Resident, District, and Provincial Engineers.

"7. Non-employment of Natives. We think, Sir, that the time has arrived in the Government of this country, when, to inspire confidence, competent and worthy natives may be appointed to important administrative positions in the Service.

"8. Municipal Government. Under this head we beg to bring to your Excellency's notice that what the country wants at the present time is an amendment of the Town Councils Ordinance so as to make the management thereof thoroughly representative. The Town Council as now constituted is unsatisfactory to, and unpopular with, the people.

"9. Education. It is much to be deplored that up to the present the Government has not established any Secondary Schools in the Colony. What is required to encourage movement of the people themselves is the founding of scholarships on the lines of the petition presented by the people in connection with the King Edward Memorial Scholarship.

"10. (a) Axim. We have, on this occasion, with us the representatives of the Axim Branch of our Society, and we desire on their behalf, to draw your Excellency's particular attention to the gradual and steady encroachment of the sea on the Amamfikuma portion of Upper Town, Axim.

"(b) Recently a Branch of the Society has been instituted at James Town, Accra; and on behalf of its members, we are to bring to your Excellency's notice that the constant proclamation of outbreak of plague is much to be deplored, as it disorganises business and is a source of much inconvenience to the people, and that preventive measures might be taken.

"We have the honour to be your Excellency's most obedient humble servants.

J. P. BROWN, *President.*
W. E. PIETERSEN, *ex-President.*
T. F. E. JONES, *Senior Vice-President.*
J. E. BINEY, *Vice-President.*
W. COLEMAN, *Vice-President.*
J. D. ABRAHAM, *Treasurer.*
GEORGE AMISSAH, *Financial Secretary.*
ATTOH-AHUMA, *Secretary.*
W. S. JOHNSTON, *Asst.-Secretary.*
C. J. BARTELS, *Kyiami.*

"To His Excellency,

"SIR HUGH CHARLES CLIFFORD, K.C.M.G., KNIGHT COMMANDER OF SAINT MICHAEL AND SAINT GEORGE, GOVERNOR AND COMMANDER-IN-CHIEF OF THE GOLD COAST COLONY AND PROTECTORATE.

"Your Excellency,

"Following our welcome address to your Excellency on the 15th instant, we respectfully beg to submit for your favourable consideration the following Memorandum.

" 1. Water Supply. This matter has been taken up by the Government in favour of Accra and Seccondee. We beg to submit that the same attention should be paid to Cape Coast. With the exception of water collected in tanks by well-to-do people, the water used in the town for drinking purposes is brackish; and the Sweet River, which we suggest might be used in this connection, is nearer Cape Coast than are the rivers to Accra and Seccondee, which are being utilised for these two places.

"2.   Transport Facilities.   Having regard to the
rapid increase in the number of cocoa plantations to
the North and North-East of this town, we pray that
facilities might be given to us for the conveyance of
produce in the shape of cocoa, palm oil, palm
kernels, kola, rubber, &c., to it.   In the Government
Gazette No. 40, page 464, dated 29th June, 1907,
His Excellency Governor Rodger, on the occasion of
the opening of the Agricultural Show at Cape Coast,
thus delivered himself.   "If planting development
warrants the necessary expenditure, a Government
railway should eventually be constructed to connect
with Cape Coast and the planting districts of the
interior, similar to the line which is about to be
constructed from Accra."   Says Mr. J. T. Furley,
Commissioner Central Province, in his report on the
Central Province for the year 1911, Gazette No. 55,
August 10, 1912, under the head of agriculture.

"'The principal feature under this head was the
rapid increase throughout the Province in the cultivation of cocoa.   Large areas are now planted, and each
year further extensions are being made.   A number of
the plantations have reached the bearing stage, and
the production will increase from year to year.   More
cocoa was produced during the year than would be
handled, and owing to lack of transport, quantities
were left ungathered on the farm.'

"Had we these facilities we are praying for, we
assure your Excellency the report of export from this
place hitherto would have been far more encouraging.

"The Cape Coast—Prahsu and Cape Coast—Jukwa
Roads, have been undergoing improvements.   We
beg to say that the work has not proceeded with that
rapidity which, from the start, we were led to expect;
and we respectfully venture to hope that greater
attention will be paid to them, and furthermore that
the Jukwa Road will be extended to Mbraim.

"If your Excellency ask us what sort of conveyance we require, we will respectfully answer a light railway.

"3. Break-water. About this, there is a long-standing promise yet unredeemed. This question was mooted when not even a cask of oil or a bag of kernals or cocoa was shipped from this port. But what do we see now, your Excellency? Steamers call here weekly for produce. Therefore, we say that this unredeemed promise should now be fulfilled. And we believe that if your Excellency will consult really competent engineers you will find that the cost will not be as great as at Seccondee or Accra.

"For the present, we confine ourselves to these as our most-keenly-felt wants, fully confident that as times goes on your Excellency will lend us a sympathetic ear to any further requirements that we may call your attention to.

"Praying for your Excellency long life, health, and success.

We beg to remain, &c.,

his

(Signed) KOFI SAKYI   ×

mark.

Regent.

& Others.

3.

"THE ABORIGINES' BANQUET.

" In Honour of His Excellency Sir Hugh Charles Clifford, K.C.M.G., Governor and Commander-in-Chief Gold Coast Colony and Protectorate.

"The banquet given to His Excellency the Governor by the Officers and Members of the Executive Committee of the Gold Coast Aborigines' Rights Protection Society, on Monday, the 19th day of May, 1913, at the District Commissioner's Court Room, Cape Coast Castle, was a brilliant success from start to finish. Covers were laid for over 80 guests, and among those who attended were the Governor's suite, viz., Captain Dalrymple, A.D.C., Mr. Holme, private secretary, Dr. C. V. Lefanu, J. T. Furley, Esq., Commissioner of the Central Province, and L. W. S. Long, Esq., District Commissioner, Cape Coast. Rev. W. R. Griffin, Chairman and Superintendent of Wesleyan Missions; Dr. Hamilton, M.O.; Captain Harrison, the Officer Commanding; Mr. Carasoy, T. & Lighterage Co.; Father Meder, Superior and Pro-Vicar of the Catholic Mission; Dr. Beringer, Medical Officer of Health; Rev. R. Fisher, M.A., S.P.G. Mission; Mr. F. S. Allen, manager, Bank of British West Africa; Mr. and Mrs. A. J. E. Bucknor, Barrister-at-law; Mr. Chatfield, Engineer of Roads; Mr. D. Palk, Provincial Engineer; Mr. Smith, Inspector of Customs; Mr. Philip, Agent, Messrs. F. & A. Swanzy; Mr. Harrison, Assistant Commissioner of Police; Sisters Mabel Robinson and Winifred Haigh, of the Girls' High School and Training Home; Mr. J. A. Barbour James, Surveyor of Post Office; Mr. A. Firman Blackmore, Headmaster Government Schools; Mr. and Mrs. Casely Hayford, Barrister-at-Law; Mr. J. L. Minnow, I.S.O.; Mrs. Eva Amissah; Mrs. J. E. Eminsang; T. F. E. Jones, Esq., Vice-President, G.C.A.R.P. Society; J. E. Biney, Esq., Vice-President, G.C.A.R.P. Society; J. R. Abraham, Esq., Treasurer, G.C.A.R.P. Society; Mrs. Esuman-Gwira; Rev. S. J. Gibson, B.Sc., of the Richmond College and Mfantsipim School; Mrs. D. Myles Abadoo; Mr. and Mrs. J. D. Aaku; Mr. G. E. Warner, of Messrs. H. B. W. Russell & Co.; Prince Atta Amonoo, Barrister-at-Law; Rev. Attoh-Ahuma, M.A., Secretary, G.C.A.R.P. Society; Rev. and Mrs.

E. A. Pinanko, Zion Mission; Mrs. G. H. Savage;
William Coleman, Esq., Vice-President, G.C.A.R.P.
Society; Mr. K. E. Asaam, Sub-Assistant Treasurer;
Mr. and Mrs. J. Bessa Simons; Mr. J. P. H. Brown,
proprietor of the *Gold Coast Leader;* Mr. E. Tagoe;
E. J. P. Brown, Esq., Barrister-at-Law; Mr. S. R.
Wood, Secretary Axim Section G.C.A.R.P. Society;
Mr. J. E. Kitson; Mr. J. A. Abadoo, Kyiami, Axim
Section G.C.A.R.P. Society; Messrs. W. Bonso
Bruce; Alexander Bruce, J. A. Mills, and Nee Lamp-
tey—representatives of the Accra Branch,
G.C.A.R.P. Society; Mr. and Mrs. E. H. Brew;
Messrs. Millers, Ltd.; Josiah Mills, Esq.; Mr. J.
E. Sagoe; Mr. John Intsiful; Mr. J. W. DeGraft
Johnson; Mr. A. D. Wilson, Kyiami of the Society.

"The Dining Hall was beautifully lit with incandes-
cent lamps of 1,500 candle power; the decorations
were simple but tasteful and effective, and
everything went on merrily as marriage bells.
Punctually at 7.30 p.m. the room was filled,
His Excellency and suite being present. Prayers
were said by the Rev. W. R. Griffin, Chairman and General Superintendent of the Wesleyan Mission, and the company sat down to discuss
a most sumptuous dinner. The menu consisted of
Hors D'œuvre varies; Soup, Fish, Entrees, Joints,
Releve, Cold Buffet, Entrements with the usual
accompaniments befitting the occasion. The wine
list was choice and select. The service left nothing
to be desired, thanks to the strenuous efforts of
Messrs. W. S. Johnston, the Assistant Secretary, and
Mr. J. Bessa Simons, Convener of the Banquet Committee, ably assisted by Mr. J. E. Sagoe, Mr. C. J.
Bartels, Mr. C. E. Graves, Messrs. J. A. Stewart,
John Intsisful, Webber and Stewart. At a quarter-
past 10 o'clock or thereabouts President J. P. Brown,
of the Aborigines' Society, who acted as Chairman of

the evening, called for order, and presented the toast of "Their Majesties the King and Queen of Great Britain and Ireland, and the Dominions beyond the Seas," which was enthusiastically honoured. The second toast was that of "Our Distinguished Guest," proposed by Casely Hayford, Esq., Barrister-at-Law, in these felicitous terms.

"Mr. Chairman, Sir Hugh Clifford, Ladies and Gentlemen. It is with pleasure that I rise to propose the toast of our distinguished guest, Sir Hugh Charles Clifford, and I wish particularly to associate with that toast the name of Lady Clifford, who we all wish could have been here with us this evening joining in this festivity. Lady Clifford's name is a household word wherever the English language is spoken, and wherever good literature is read and appreciated.

"My introduction to the works of Lady Clifford was somewhat in this wise. When coming down here on the boat with my wife the other day, she had a touch of sea-sickness. It was not the type that our good and mutual friend Dr. Lefanu would style virulent. Still, it was bad enough while it lasted. I made her comfortable, and then went away for a bit. When I returned she was reading a book. She seemed content. I did not want to disturb her. When I came back again she was still reading it, and she did not stop till she had finished reading it. It was one of Lady Clifford's books. It was nearly dusk now. I took the book in my hands, turned over the pages, and said "I see." Well—I took possession of the book, and I can assure you that not even a decree of the Aborigines' Society will make me part with that book till I have read it from cover to cover.

"My wife forbids me referring to Sir Hugh Clifford's works in the same breath as Lady Clifford's. Still, I cannot resist the temptation of saying I knew His Excellency before I had the honour of meeting him on the Gold Coast. It was through his books. I am not going to satisfy your curiosity by telling you which. You must find out for yourself. I as it were reserved my judgment. I said some day I might meet His Excellency. Well, I came, I saw; you have come and you have seen in him, as in his books, an earnestness and a consciousness which, enlisted in the service of any human activity, must command success and the admiration of men.

"The assembly here to-night, Sir, reminds one of the days of the judicial assessors. There was a time when the officers of the Government mixed freely with the people. I believe the Eastern Province provided an African Governor in the person of the late James Bannerman. The judicial assessors sat on the Bench with native chiefs, and we had principal medical officers of African descent. Those times, after a while, seemed to have gone past. Then we come to a period of isolation, of distrust, of segregation, and even of suspicion.

"We bridge over the gulf of time and come to the year 1913 in the month of May. His Excellency has told us that we must not expect that he is going to create for us a new heaven and a new earth. But we know what he is going to do, that he will restore the confidence of the people in a way that has not been done since the days of Governor Maclean. He was able to inspire the sympathy and the loyalty of the people, and he ruled with a success that has scarcely been matched since.

"The Aborigines' Society has been doing a good work, in reviving the confidence of the people. You know we cannot help people thinking, and I think it is safe for all concerned to know what they are thinking about, and for this reason an intelligent press, dignified in tone, is a useful thing and so a body like the Aborigines' Society which interprets the needs and the wants of the people.

"There is a force in this country which we are apt to make little of and do not appreciate sufficiently. I refer to the warm-heartedness, the loyalty and the devotion of the people to any administration or official in whom they have confidence. I must confess, Sir, that when in the Seccondee address we suggested that your Excellency might be pleased to extend your tour to the Central Province and to this historic town, we were nervous lest you might not be able to do so. Seeing the enthusiasm of the people, one may say your Excellency has been repaid for the trouble you have taken. One characteristic act of a characteristic man has blotted out the memory of the past and restored the confidence, the sympathy, and the co-operation of the people.

"But co-operation, Mr. Chairman, ladies, and gentlemen, must be intelligent, frank, and earnest, otherwise it helps not on the work intended ; and, so, we bespeak for the new administration such co-operation.

"Two notable thoughts have been contributed to political literature quite recently. The one is by Lord Rosebery, where he points to Japan as an object-lesson of national efficiency. That is relevant in so far as it enables us to appreciate also the success of Japan in colonising. For the second thought is by Baron Goto, where he refers to the Formosans as Fellow Nationals. That suggests training the Formosan people to the status of citizenship. It precludes the idea of their being for ever hewers of wood and drawers of water. It is unfortunate that that exactly has not appeared to be the object of a recent administration. We hope to see revived in the time of the present administration the ideal of citizenship, so that the people of this country may take their true place as citizens of the British Empire.

"One thought more, and I have done. We thank His Excellency for the assurance as regards our lands that the pledges given to us by Mr. Chamberlain will not be set at naught nor our right to them in any way interfered with.

"Sir, our land system and our institutions are founded upon a rock, and we trust they will find in your Excellency a sure defence. In that hope and in that faith I wish your Excellency and your consort long life, success, and prosperity in the administration of this country. I ask you all to drink heartily the health of His Excellency and Lady Clifford.

"On rising to respond Sir Hugh received a grand ovation.

"His Excellency the Governor, in responding to the toast in his honour, said he must begin by thanking the Society for the warm reception and grand entertainment that had been accorded him that night. Mr. Hayford had begun his speech with kind reference to Lady Clifford. He regretted that on that occasion of his first visit to Cape Coast, he was alone, but he hoped that upon the next opportunity when he could pay another visit to our ancient town, Lady Clifford would be with him. He felt proud to hear from Mr. Hayford that Mrs. Hayford's " sea sickness " on board the " Burutu " on the voyage to this town last week had been relieved by one of Lady Clifford's books which she happened to be reading at that time. His Excellency added that during the last few weeks, he had received many letters from several parts of the Empire, to whom Lady Clifford's books had brought comfort, enquiring anxiously after her health. It was sad to record that none of his own books had ever been known to soothe the pangs of sea-sickness, though he had been told that certain passages in some of them sometimes occasioned a feeling of nausea.

"Speaking to the Society, His Excellency said he should like to thank the President, Officers, and members thereof for entertaining him so lavishly that night. Only one circumstance could have rendered the compliment paid to him more complete, and that would be if the entertainment had been given to him at the end of five years among them instead of after a period of only five months' administration of the Government of that Colony. He trusted that the cordiality which had prevailed at the commencement of his administration would remain intact during the course of his tenure of office. No one was more convinced than himself of the impossibility to please everyone, and in illustrating this, His Excellency referred to the story of the man, the donkey, and his son, who, by listening to the conflicting advice of various people ended in finding themselves in a river. All that a man could do in the administration of such a Colony as that was to devote all his energies to the task of learning from those whose local knowledge entitled them to be heard. Here His Excellency referred to Sir Walter Scott, and said that even he, a man of such large reputation and learning, used to say that he never spent ten minutes in the company of anyone without learning something he did not know before. After serving for 30 years in other parts of the Empire, he had now come to live under entirely new conditions and amid an entirely new environment, and his first duty therefore was to learn about the country from personal observation. The main object of the present tour was to enable him to come in contact with the representatives of the various interests in the Colony, to discuss and exchange views with them, for therein lay the safest route to that knowledge without which it would not be possible for him materially to enhance the prosperity of this country. He knew he could not satisfy all parties ; he was not able to meet the wishes of everyone—for instance, even some of the modest requests recently made to him by some of the merchants at Cape Coast ; but he promised everyone a patient and courteous hearing who had any matter to lay before him. His Excellency emphasized the point that, a man who made no mistakes made nothing. On certain occasions his judgment might be betrayed and he might make mistakes which he would regret afterwards. All he could promise was that, no mistake would be made knowingly ; he claimed no infallibility of judgment; for that was not an attribute of humanity, but he would administer the affairs of this country to the best of his conscience and strive to rule it as God would have him rule it. Finally he would thank the people of this ancient town once more for the warm reception that had been accorded him; his sensations would be devoid of gratitude did he not again take the opportunity to thank the people. He had visited Elmina that day, where he had also been accorded a hearty, and he might perhaps be permitted to add—a noisy welcome. The streets were somewhat narrow and very crowded, when to this was added the unceasing detonation of guns his feelings had been divided between gratitude for a warm reception and a splitting headache. This must serve as his excuse if his speech that evening disappointed his audience.

"His Excellency, in conclusion, said he wished again to thank that great Society for the sumptuous banquet and entertainment of that evening, and also to express the hope that the good feelings which had that night been manifested might continue unchanged throughout the whole period of his administration.

" Then the Rev. S. J. Gibson, B.Sc. (Lond.), Acting Principal of the Mfantsipim School and Richmond College, gave the toast of " The Gold Coast Aborigines' Rights Protection Society."—Mr. Gibson said :—

" It is a grand thing when a people recognises that it has a heritage of ancestral rights ; when it feels that the past is not a nameless, shameful shadow, and realises that its forefathers have in the long, long years evolved a system of customs and usages which are trustworthy, practicable and expedient in the economy and polity of the present. There is always the possibility that new legislative measures may be proposed which, however sincere may be the promoters, laws and customs on which the social fabric of our law is based. To prevent these is the object and aim of the Society which entertains us to-night, for it seeks to preserve the old, not because of its antiquity but because of its intrinsic value.

" Through always being in a position of criticising the weak and attacking the false there is a danger that due praise would not be given to the true and a possibility of such a Society degenerating into a permanent opposition, we can all congratulate this Society on the even balance which typifies both its words and its actions. We appreciate not only the dignity and fearlessness which has always characterised its attack on what it feels to be false, but also the charity and forbearance with which it has treated its opponents and the welcome which it always has offered to that which is good and true.

" We all of us recognise that all true and lasting reforms must be first internal.

" Tribes and factions can only be transformed into a nation from within. That is the principle which actuated the founders of this Society.

" The aim and to a great extent the achievement of the Society, is the union of what I may term the acidic and basic radicals of the Gold Coast into a compound of sweetness and stability. The attention which the Society has given to such side issues as commerce, especially agriculture, education, with particular reference to secondary education, and journalism, with regards to their official organ, which is an honest attempt to supply a journal free from those blemishes which so often disfigure colonial newspapers, all these show the sincerity and wisdom of its members.

" It would hardly be my desire to wish this Society long life. I hope that it will never succumb to senile decay, or to that chest complaint associated with West African currency, but that, its objects being attained, it will be enabled to retire gracefully when by reason of an amended constitution, the Aborigines Rights are adequately advocated in that governing body which is so largely responsible for our welfare. I ask you all to be upstanding and to drink ' Success and Prosperity to the Gold Coast Aborigines' Rights Protection Society.''

"In response to this toast the Rev. S. R. B. Attoh-Ahuma, M.A., the Secretary of the Society, thus delivered himself :—

"May it please your Excellency, ladies and gentlemen,

"The proposer of this toast has often amused me by calling himself an '' adopted Aborigine,'' and all

who have just heard him will no doubt agree with me
when I say that if he had been bone of our bone and
flesh of our flesh, he could not have done better in
presenting the work and worth of the Aborigines'
Society.   In the name and on behalf of the officers
and members of the parent Society and the branches
at Axim and Accra respectively, therefore, I thank the
Rev. Gibson for the eloquent manner in which he has
proposed the toast in question and you ladies and
gentlemen for the enthusiastic reception you have so
generously accorded it.   I must premise by saying
how overwhelmed we are by the most favourable
remarks that fell from the lips of His Excellency in
the course of his splendid and instructive speech with
respect to the Society.   We owe a deep debt of
gratitude to the Governor for his good opinion of us.
It is very much to be regretted that after the lapse
of fifteen years it should be at all necessary to dis-
abuse the minds of people in certain quarters who still
maintain that the Gold Coast Aborigines' Rights Protection Society exists for the sole purpose of opposing
all legislative measures emanating from His Majesty's
Government right or wrong.   That is not a fact.
Others seem to harbour the idea that its members are
more or less influenced by a morbid love of cheap
notoriety, and some even go the length of presuming
that it is with the object of self-advertisement that
they meet week after week, year in, year out.   No,
your Excellency, ladies and gentlemen, the Society
exists to disseminate the principles of true citizenship,
and it is the earnest endeavour of its members to be
only useful in the service of their home and country.
We are proud, therefore, to think that the Governor
has no share in the opinion and judgment of our
traducers.   I can assure you that we are actuated
by no unworthy or sinister motives; with the very
best intentions and with hearts sincere we live to do
all the good we can to the sons and daughters of the

soil. We have not impeded and we do not impede the advancement of the Government in any shape or form; on the other hand, we have in some notable instances accelerated and do still try to accelerate it. The Society has never done anything antagonistic to the good Government of the country since its inauguration 15 years ago. Another point that must be submitted is the unwarranted assumption that the Society originated with and is engineered by a band of educated men in the community. That also is not a fact. There are no professional patriots in the Society. The personnel of this political organisation consists of gentlemen some of whom have in their own right reversionary interests in the Stools occupied by the ruling Kings and Chiefs of the day, while others are closely related to them; consequently, it would be suicidal for any of them to do anything out of harmony with the true spirit of national advancement. This, however, does not preclude them from vehemently opposing any measure that in the opinion of members is detrimental to the customary rights and usages of the people they represent, or is subversive of the traditions and privileges of the country. In the Declaration of Constitution are recorded the origin and the specific aims and objects of the Society. Sir Frederick Mitchell Hodgson, K.C.M.G., was the first to extend to us the right hand of fellowship within the precincts of this very Castle, and subsequent Governors have not been backward in recognising the usefulness of the Society. Whatever doubts and suspicions lurked in the minds of our opponents should have been completely set at rest by the emphatic pronouncement of Mr. Special Commissioner Belfield, when in Paragraph 152 of his report—copies of which you gentlemen, I trust, have secured—he absolutely exonerates the educated members of the Executive Committee. Our Bye-Laws are based on the principles I have already referred to.

I challenge anyone here to-night to say aught against the integrity of the Aborigines' Society; these principles of sympathy, goodwill, and kindly consideration it is our honest intention to strictly adhere to. If this were a Court of Justice I should like to put the District Commissioner and the Provincial Commissioner into the witness box, and then your Excellency and you, ladies and gentlemen, shall be convinced that the Aborigines' Rights Protection Society has not been a negligible quantity in the political affairs at least of the Central Province during their tenure of office. The Society is a force to reckon with; until our Commissioners and other officers in authority became absolutely familiar with the idiosyncracies, customs, laws, habits and modes of thought peculiar to the native, until they knew what it is to *think black*, as Miss Kingsley puts it, the Aborigines' Society shall ever remain a force to reckon with in the administration of the Government of this Colony and Protectorate. The Society has stood for, stands for, and shall always stand for, strenuous effort to ensure combination of the scattered interests and the unity of our natural Rulers; the establishment of harmonious relations one with the other and the cohesion of forces which make for the safety of the public and the welfare of the race. Mr. Gibson has referred in flattering terms to the efforts of the official organ of the Society; as the officer responsible for that department of our work, I must express my regrets for two reasons; first, that vernacular training has not sufficiently advanced to admit of the publication of the Society's journal in Fanti so as to secure the widest possible circulation. Secondly, English being an acquired language, it is possible that we may not have succeeded in giving adequate expression to our views and opinion in ventilating the grievances and requirements of our constituency; the little we have been able to do, however, has met with the kind approval of eminent men among us; on the authority of the Rev. Griffin who, I am glad to find, has so far recovered from his recent illness to be at His Excellency's table to-night; on the authority of Bishop Hummel, of the Catholic Mission, who, I regret to state, is away to Europe on furlough; on the authority of the Principal of the Richmond College, and from the casual words to which the Governor gave utterance last Friday when the members of the Executive Committee had an interview with him, and when His Excellency graciously referred to certain temperate articles that had appeared in the *Nation*, we feel encouraged and enheartened to go forward in the thorny path of journalism in West Africa; and we promise you that so long as we are connected with the Society's official organ no scurrilous contribution shall find accommodation in its columns. Finally, we indulge the hope that when Sir Hugh has studied the Society from every point of view, and has satisfied himself of its merits and capabilities His Excellency would be pleased to make the Gold Coast Aborigines' Rights Protection Society the authorised channel for the practical realisation of that frank co-operation which he seeks."

"Our Natural Rulers" was proposed by T. F. E. Jones, Esq., Senior Vice-President, in these words:

"Your Excellency, Ladies and Gentlemen,—With great pleasure I rise to propose the toast of 'Our Natural Rulers.' But I am afraid, Mr. President, the Chairman of this function has made a wrong choice in calling me to rise to propose the toast, as I am not fluent in English speaking, which to me is an acquired language. I shall, however, try to do the best I can.

"Our Natural Rulers have always been the instruments in the hands of the Government for the administration of the Colony and Protectorate. They have always been assiting the Government in every direction. This hall has been generally known as 'The Palaver Hall.' Although there is doubt as to whether palaver is an English word, yet it is generally understood to mean a cause or matter, hence palaver hall was known to be where matters or causes of civil and criminal nature as well as political were adjudicated by the Judicial Assessor together with our Natural Rulers. In case of legislation, the Governor convened a meeting of them all to come to Cape Coast to confer with them before any law was passed, when each ruler carried with him such law and caused a Gong-Gong to be beaten in his Division for the information of his subjects. What do we see now? Instead of the beating of Gong-Gong through the medium of our Natural Rulers as before stated, the Government seems to think that the publication of any new law in the Government Gazette is sufficient notification to the public, not considering that the number of those who could read and write in this country is less than about five per cent.

" Laws are every now and again passed without their knowledge and usual co-operation, hence the absolute ignorance of themselves and their subjects of any new legislation, until he himself or his subject has been charged with a breach of same, when it is explained to him in the dock.

" We hope it will not be so during your administration, so that the ancient co-operation (if dead) might be resuscitated. Our present Natural Rulers are the successors of those who were parties to the ' Bond of 1844 ' in which document they conferred a part of their inherent Criminal Jurisdiction to her late Majesty the Queen of England.

" But for the assistance of our Natural Rulers, how difficult would it have been for the Government to quietly govern the masses? There would have been a necessity to station District Commissioners all over the hinterland, and consider the amount of revenue that might be required to do so.

" We further hope that your Excellency will find your way to take our said Natural Rulers into your confidence in the administration of this country.

" I beg to again ask you all to drink the health of our Natural Rulers."

"Responding, E. J. P. Brown, Esq., Barrister-at-Law, spoke as follows :—

"Your Excellency, Mr. President, Officers and Members, Ladies and Gentlemen,—

" In thanking you in the name and on behalf of our Natural Rulers, whose toast you have just honoured, I beg to explain one circumstance in connection with this pleasant gathering, and that is the absence of our Natural Rulers. They are unable to be present to-night owing to a rigid rule of native etiquette which forbids their partaking food in public. At this period of the evening I do not intend to inflict upon you a very lengthy speech. In fact, this is not the time for a political speech, but I feel a temptation to refer to certain historical facts whose association with this hall and the present gathering deserves mention. This is the historic Palaver Hall, as was told you by the last speaker, in which had met the predecessors of our Natural Rulers and previous Governors of this Colony and Protectorate for the deliberation of political matters, the enactment of laws, and the trial of political offenders.

" Our Native Rulers acted as judges and legislators, the Governor sitting with them as President. It was in this historic hall that the celebrated Governor Maclean, conjointly with some of the forbears of our Kings and Chiefs, made a Treaty with the King of Ashanti, which defined, for the first time, the extent of British jurisdiction in this country. The famous Bond of 1844, whereby the forbears of our Natural Rulers conferred certain jurisdictional rights in criminal cases on the British Government, was also signed in this very hall. Speaking of the Bond of 1844 reminds me of the opinion which I once heard a Government official (not in the Service now) express—' The Bond of 1844 is now obsolete,' he said. That is not true, for were that so, the British Government would have no footing in this country. The Bond of 1844 has subsequently been supplemented and emphasised by the Native Jurisdiction Ordinance—a regulative measure, placing on a proper basis the inherent jurisdictional rights of our Native Rulers. Eight years after the signing of the Bond, the people of this country, as the allies of the British Government, sent a combined expedition against the notorious King Kweku Akai to punish him for his fiendish atrocities and studied defiance to British authority. He was captured, tried, found guilty, and sentenced to death in this very hall by the Kings and Chiefs and the Governor as President, but his sentence was commuted to that of penal servitude for life; he died in 1852. It was also in this hall that the first legislative meeting, composed of the forbears of our Natural Rulers and the Governor took place when, in order to carry on the Government of the country, sanction was given to the British Government by the Kings and Chiefs to impose customs duties for the establishment of schools, the erection of works of public utility, and the increase of the judiciary.

" The Aborigines' Society is composed of our Natural Rulers, the officers and members present here to-night being the Executive Body, carrying out the wishes and directions of our Natural Rulers. The present gathering, therefore, forms a happy link in the chain of unbroken friendship and loyalty of the people of this Country towards the good British People which our Natural Rulers recall with just pride and pleasure. Having thus taken an equal part in the administration of this Country, our Natural Rulers recently addressed a petition to His Majesty the King, praying for a restoration to their former position in the way of fuller representation on the Legislative Council. For some reason or other His Majesty would not be advised to alter the present system. Your Excellency has asked for a free, frank, and cordial co-operation from our Natural Rulers, which they are prepared now and always to give to Your Excellency, but there can be no better and surer way of giving full effect to such co-operation than by giving them a proper voice in the government of the Country. It may be urged that there is now on the Legislative Council one of our Natural Rulers, namely, Konor Mate Kole. But as far as I am informed, he is there representing agricultural interests in accordance with the expressed wish of the late Governor, Sir J. P. Rodger, when he rightly recommended that owing to the growing importance of the agricultural community, its interests should be assured in the form of a representative on the Legislative Council. His appointment, therefore, on the death of the late Honourable Sarbah was obviously not to fill the place left vacant by the deceased member, but to create a new membership altogether.

" Your Excellency's varied career in the East and other parts of the British Empire, where the preservation of the integrity of Native States is the primary object of the Government, convinces us that during Your Excellency's administration our Natural Rulers will once more be made to take their proper share in the administration of this Country as was done in the days of our forbears.

" Our Natural Rulers are working together for the solidarity of national aims, and although in the days of the

Fanti Confederation (between 1867 and 1872) much discouragement and strong opposition were brought to bear on the efforts of our forbears to establish for themselves lasting foundations for self-government, to-day an enlightened Administration is on the fair way of making amends for the mistakes of a former administration by the very sympathetic recognition it has given, and still continues to give, to the Gold Coast Aborigines' Rights Protection Society— an offspring of the famous but short-lived Fanti Confederation. In conclusion, it is gratifying to observe that the present occasion evidences a state of things which is eloquent of the fact that our Natural Rulers are in unity, and that unity is in the Country for the prosperity and well-being of all concerned."

"The last toast on the list was safely placed in the hands of Tufuhin Kobina Ayensu (Chief W. Z. Coker).

TOAST, GOLD COAST COLONY AND PROTECTORATE.

" I have been asked to travel within a very wide area of about 82,000 square miles, with a population of nearly three million people, who are ruled by their Natural Rulers— Amanhin, Ahinfu, Mantseme, Konor, Seriki, Fia, &c., &c., and all these Natural Rulers are under the protection of the wisest colonisers—the British Government. The Gold Coast was first discovered by the Phœnicians many years before the birth of Christ, and we traded with them in gold and aggrey beads. Since then we have had intercourse with Europe, and have been exporting gold dust and other products. Each year the exports have been increasing by leaps and bounds. The British Government has had communication with us for the last 200 years, and it was only during the time that Mr. Chamberlain took office as Secretary of State for the Colonies that the Gold Coast was brought into prominence before the British public as one of the valuable estates of the British Crown. There is vast and unlimited wealth in the Colony—rubber, timber, cocoa, palm-oil, palm-kernels, kola-nuts, &c., and I believe we have also diamonds, if we could only get experts to trace them.

" Our difficulty is transport. What we require is transport facilities, and if we get these facilities from the hinterland to the coast, I think the Gold Coast will in a few years be one of the richest estates in the British Empire. The Gold

Coast, as you all know, especially those who have seen the gold mines, have noted the vast wealth with which it abounds, and I am sure that in a few years we will be shipping not only gold, but also diamonds.

" In conclusion, I submit to you the toast of ' The Gold Coast Colony and Protectorate.' "

"The Provincial Commissioner, in responding, referred to the present position of the Colony as a most important one in the British Empire. The country was an extensive territory. During the previous year the Gold Coast beat the record in the quantity of cocoa shipped for the European markets from the various cocoa producing centres. He wished for the country greater success and prosperity.

"The Governor briefly proposed the health of J. P. Brown, Esq., the Chairman, and said how successful the evening's function had been, trusting that the great Society might have success, long life, and prosperity. After President Brown had replied in suitable terms, and had assured the company that as long as he lived his services would always be at the disposal of his country, the anthem of the Empire, " God save the King," was lustily sung, and a most enjoyable evening was brought to a close.

4

" MEMORANDUM OF REQUIREMENTS AND GRIEVANCES OF THE RATEPAYERS OF CAPE COAST RESPECTFULLY SUBMITTED BY THE UNOFFICIAL MEMBERS FOR THE KIND CONSIDERATION OF HIS EXCELLENCY THE GOVERNOR.

"*Water Supply.* The question of water supply is a sore one. About two years ago it was proposed by the Government to send an expert to Cape Coast to test areas between the hills in the town with a view to creating spring tanks as reservoirs for a general water supply. This scheme was never carried out

General Drainage. This should be on a more improved and extensive scale. For example, the main drain requires widening, deepening, or raising the walls on the sides to allow a free flow of the large volume of water which overflows its banks and does considerable damage to adjacent houses during the rainy season. There are also many by-way drains in the town which require immediate attention. Some of the streets also require attention.

Town Surveyor. The appointment of an Engineer or Surveyor for the Council independently of the Public Works Department to facilitate the work of the Council, demands immediate attention.

Native Club House. A Native Club House, combining a Town Hall for the Municipality to be managed and conducted by the Council is urgently required to meet the pressing social needs of the people. Accra and Seccondee have Native Club Houses.

Building Regulations. These have been carried out by the Council officials without consulting and obtaining the sanction of the Council. Demolition of houses and refusal of permits for buildings take place as by " Orders of the Council " when the Council, as a matter of fact, had not met and given such directions. No discretion is also exercised with respect to the discretionary provision in the Towns Ordinance, the exercise of the powers of which is vested in the Town Council by Section 38 (1) of the Town Councils Ordinance No. 17 of 1894.

Housing Problem. The principal objection of the Official Members is with respect to swish buildings. It is an admitted fact that the Cape Coast swish is the strongest in the country. Even at Axim, where the swish is not of much strength for building purposes, a departure has been made in the Regulations to allow the people to build their houses with swish. There are swish houses in this town built since the seventeenth century which are still in good condition. There is no opposition to any suggestion as to ventilation, &c., and the proper planning of houses; what the people desire is that they should be allowed to build with swish as heretofore on sanitary principles. It may not be out of place to suggest that in the case of a whole locality, where the people have been asked to give up their houses, ample compensation should be paid to enable them to acquire suitable sites to build on. Lest it may be feared that the moneys so paid to owners of demolished houses may not be utilised for building purposes, it is respectfully suggested that all moneys paid under such circumstances be deposited in the bank by the Council, on the owner's behalf, and builders contracted for at a reasonable estimate to build houses on approved sanitary plans. Any balance to be paid to the owners after completion of the buildings.

Enforcement of Sanitary Measures. In enforcing sanitary measures, although firmness in action is necessary, yet sympathy with a view to getting the people to realise the benefit to be derived, ought to be shown by the Sanitary officials. For example, where a nuisance complained of has been abated before the expiration of the notice, people have been summoned and fined for the same nuisance. Owing to the want of kindly consideration on the part of Sanitary officials in dealing with sanitary questions, the people have come to regard the Town Council as a medium for oppression in the name of sanitary improvements.

Town Council unpopular with the people. The people are not enamoured of the Town Council as at present constituted. When it was first extended to this town the people objected to it as a quasi-Government institution under executive control by reason of the President being always an official and also the preponderance of official over unofficial votes. Until some time in 1906, the people refused to elect members to the Council. However, as the promise was held out to them that the Council was instituted to train them in the system of self-government, and that upon showing efficiency in the matter the Council would be given over to them to manage and conduct for their benefit, they elected their own representatives to see how far that promise would be carried out. Since then, the views of the Unofficial Members of the Council have been given little or no attention. While one President sympathetically inclines to the views of the Unofficial Members, his successor takes no notice of them. The constant changes of officials, owing to the present leave system of the Civil Service, makes it impossible to secure continuity of policy—consequently the Town Council has not been a success. Not satisfied with the present condition of things, the people refused to return members to the Council at the last election, with the result that the Governor nominated the present Unofficial Members.

Substantial Subvention to the Town Council. Owing to the commercial depression of the town through the introduction of railways in the Eastern and Western Provinces, and the consequent diversion of its trade routes, the value of houses has gone down, many houses being untenanted. The people have great difficulty in meeting their rates, and although the percentage of 5 per cent. on the assessed rates has been reduced to 3 per cent., the present heavy areas of rates are a proof of the inability of the people to pay their rates. It is respectfully suggested that a substantial subvention be made to the

Council to enable it to effect the necessary improvements if it is so urgently required.

"The statement is reiterated that the Council as at present constituted denies the ratepayers the advantages of self-government.   It is therefore respectfully suggested that the Town Councils Ordinance requires some material amendments which should secure to the people a proper form of municipal government as was held out to them on the application of the Town Councils Ordinance to this town.

(Signed)

E. J. P. BROWN,
T. F. E. JONES,
J. D. ABRAHAM,
J. W. DE GRAFT JOHNSON,
Unofficial Members C. C. T. C.

"Your Excellency,

"We, the merchants of Cape Coast, have the honour to welcome your Excellency here, and we trust that your visit may result in the improvement of trade and conditions generally.

"We have been courteously invited by the Provincial Commissioner to lay before your Excellency our suggestions for improvements which we deem necessary.   We gladly avail ourselves of this opportunity to bring to your Excellency's notice the following :—

"I.   In order to facilitate the shipment of produce, the erection of a shed near the beach for storage purposes would be of inestimable advantage.   Messrs. the West African Lighterage and Transport Co., Ltd., are willing to bear the expense of the building, provided a suitable site be granted to them, and all difficulties would be removed if your Excellency could arrange to allot to them the open space at the base of Castle Hill, opposite the Customs beach.

II. The two approaches to the Customs beach, *via* Low Town and Castle Hill, are at present in an exceedingly bad state of repair. All imports and exports have to pass over these roads, and their permanent repair to withstand a four ton load is urgently required. Accumulations of water on the Low Town road have occasionally rendered haulage impossible.

III. It is with regret we have to point out that the telegraph service is somewhat unsatisfactory. Mutilations of telegrams and cablegrams, and delay in their delivery are of frequent occurrence, and any steps your Excellency may see fit to take to improve the local service will be greatly appreciated.

IV. The Jukwa and Prahsu roads, the only arteries for the conveyance of produce, would be greatly improved by rendering all bridges at an early date capable of permitting motor traction; more especially would we call your Excellency's attention to the bridge five miles hence on the Jukwa road, and 17 miles on the Prahsu road. It would materially benefit farmers and merchants alike were these two roads continued, that to Jukwa so as to reach Mampong, and the other main road carried from Dunkwa to Prahsu. As soon as the roads are generally in a suitable condition to sustain motor traffic, there is every reason to believe the exports from this port will very considerably increase.

V. Under existing conditions the merchants are seriously hampered by lack of space for drying cocoa before shipment. The factories cannot adequately cope with the difficulty, and we would respectfully request your Excellency's permission to utilise in this respect certain open spaces adjacent to our warehouses. We would suggest, on behalf of Messrs.

the African Association, Ltd., Millers, Ltd., and the Compagnie Francaise de l'Afrique Occidentale, the privilege of using the rectangle in Intin Street known as Watt's land; for Messrs. H. B. W. Russell & Co., a section of the Victoria Park; and for Messrs. J. J. Fischer & Co., a plot at the base of Hospital Hill.

VI.   Only cases relating to amounts of under £50 at present fall within the jurisdiction of the District Commissioner's Court.   This sum represents virtually the value of only one puncheon of rum, and a considerable rum trade is carried on in Cape Coast. It would be a distinct advantage to merchants were the limit raised to £80 or £100, and thus obviate the delay caused by waiting for hearing in the High Court.

"Expressing our thanks for the opportunity kindly accorded by your Excellency to submit our proposals, we beg to subscribe ourselves,

"For F. & A. Swanzy, T. PHILIP.
For African Association, V. HARRIS.
For Millers, Ltd., E. H. BREW.
For C. F. A. O., F. CONSTANT.
For B. B. W. A., Ltd., F. S. ALLEN.
For J. J. Fischer & Co., Ltd., J. E. HAYFORD.
For the West African Lighterage & Transport Co., J. CARASOV.

5

"THE SECCONDEE ADDRESSES TO HIS EXCELLENCY SIR HUGH CHARLES CLIFFORD, KNIGHT COMMANDER OF THE MOST DISTINGUISHED ORDER OF SAINT MICHAEL AND SAINT GEORGE, GOVERNOR AND COMMANDER-IN-CHIEF OF THE GOLD COAST COLONY.

"May it please your Excellency,

"We, the undersigned Omanhin of English Seccondee, the Omanhin of Dutch Seccondee, and others, the Councillors, Elders, Captains, and the principal native inhabitants of Seccondee as well as the Amanhin, Ahinfu (Kings and Chiefs) and others, the principal native inhabitants of Seccondee-Dixcove District, beg leave respectfully to welcome your Excellency to the Gold Coast Colony, and to Seccondee in particular, and regret the circumstances which have made it impossible for Lady Clifford to share in the hearty greeting which we bring you this day, and pray to God that He may preserve both Lady Clifford and your Excellency in good health long to administer the affairs of this Dependency.

"Your Excellency has taken up the reins of Government at a time in the history of the country when, to ensure success, it is necessary for all sections of the community to accord your Excellency frank co-operation. We are here to-day to assure your Excellency of such co-operation during your administration, and we have reason to believe that in this we echo the sincere sentiment of the whole country.

"In this connection we cannot help recalling the memorable message which her late gracious Majesty, Queen Victoria of revered memory, caused to be sent on the 17th February, 1908, to one of our Amanhin through the then Governor, in these words :—"King : —I am directed by the Acting Governor to inform you that the telegram which you and others sent to the Queen on the 21st December was duly received, and that His Excellency is commanded to state that her Majesty was pleased to receive it very graciously, and that her Majesty does not doubt that the Governor of the Gold Coast will cordially co-operate with you for the welfare and advancement of the Colony."

"Your Excellency will see that from the time of the late Queen-Empress the relations between the Crown and the people have been marked with a sincere devotion to the person of the Sovereign and loyalty to the throne. And we beg to assure your Excellency of the profound sympathy of the people in your recent anxiety as to the health of your Excellency's consort and household. We trust that it will be within the power of science to determine definitely the causes of these outbreaks, and to devise means for their prevention.

"Before your Excellency's arrival in this Dependency the record of your Excellency's enlightened official career in other parts of his Majesty's dominions beyond the seas had reached us. In dealing with the people of the Gold Coast your Excellency will come in contact with customs and institutions which may be novel, but which nevertheless have their foundation in the history and evolution of the people. From what we know of your Excellency's broadmindedness we are sure that the peculiar position of the Gold Coast will meet with due sympathy and consideration on the part of your Excellency.

"We have read with pleasure in the local press of your Excellency's successful tour in the Eastern Province, and we are convinced that the interest of the general colony will be advanced if your Excellency can make it convenient to extend your visit to other parts of the Colony, including the Central Province.

"We are, your Excellency's obedient, humble servants,

ANAISI II., Omanhin, Dutch Seccondee;

INKETSIA, Omanhin, English Seccondee;

and others.

"Seccondee,

22nd April, 1912.

" Sir,

" We, the undersigned Omanhin of Dutch Seccondee, the Omanhin of English Seccondee and others, the Councillors, Elders, Captains and the principal native inhabitants of Seccondee, beg leave through you to express to His Excellency the Governor our appreciation of the opportunity given us of laying before him our grievances and wants, and in doing so desire to assure him of our wish in all loyalty to co-operate with the local authorities in the good government of the town of Seccondee.

2. Our first grievance is with respect to the taking over of several town plots by the Government. While we recognise that for public purposes land may now and again be required by the Government, yet we must respectfully object to the taking of land intended for public purposes and afterwards Government letting out such lands to private individuals on leases.

Among instances of this in Dutch Seccondee part of the town may be mentioned the site of the premises of the Bank, Allen's Hotel, and Messrs. Swanzy's business houses, which, originally acquired on the understanding that they were required for the improvement of the town, have since been leased to the Bank, Messrs. Swanzy, and to the late W. E. Sam for substantial consideration monies and annual rentals.

3. We would point out here that if the object of the Government was to ensure good buildings being put up on the sites in question, the owners of the lands might have been given time to put up such buildings themselves or to grant leaseholds of the premises to suitable applicants, thus ensuring to themselves the rents.

We wish to point out that by the methods adopted by the Government the holders of these private lands have been deprived of the income which they might otherwise have derived from them.

4. In the acquisition of these lands by Government the owners have no option in the matter. In the particular instances cited the owners for a long time refused payment, and it was upon their apprehension that if payment was not

taken they might lose what had been offered that they were induced to accept such payment.

5. It might also be pointed out that in these Government acquisitions of town areas the owners deal with the Government at a disadvantage since there is no independent valuation, and the Government has practically the right to say how much it would give as consideration.

6. Another grievance with respect to our lands is that some of them are taken without in any way consulting the convenience of the owners or even consulting the chiefs upon the matter. The whole of the land from the Sanitary Engineer's office along Council Road to River Essa and thence on the right bank to the Central Prison and from thence to the Colonial Hospital back to the Sanitary Engineer's office was thus taken, and there has been no consideration paid for it.

These lands belong to the Stool of the Omanhin of Dutch Seccondee, and it is considered by him and his people a great hardship that they should thus be deprived of their property.

7. Further from Central Prison to Abrayaba village on the new railway line, a pillar has been fixed by the Government. We have the same objection to this area being taken without consulting the owners or their convenience.

8. Again from new British Seccondee (Essikadu) to Kojo Krome has been taken without consulting the owners or their convenience.

The people fail to see why these appropriations should be made without their consent, and beg that His Excellency may look into the matter.

9. With regard to appropriations in Dutch Seccondee, it is necessary to point out that while Government are letting out Stool lands at a rental, the chief's own people have no land to build upon.

10. We wish also to complain of the way in which the Amanhin are made to lower their dress to the waist before the Commissioner. This is contrary to custom, as all that is expected of an Omanhin in paying respects is to touch his head band and bow. The compelling of an Omanhin to lower his apparel to the waist is an act of humiliation about which the people feel deeply, and we shall be pleased if His

Excellency would direct that due consideration be given to the Amanhin.

11. The fishing people of the town would ask His Excellency to consider the question of providing them with a suitable beach for going a fishing and landing, after preventing them from using the old landing place.

They would suggest the beach from Kleinart's brick works to Accra town beach. It is a great hardship for the fishermen to have no recognised place for going off or landing.

12. The land also from Mr. Christian's bungalow to Mr. Kleinart's brick works is also taken by the Government without rent being paid to the owners.

13. Another matter which we desire to bring to His Excellency's notice is the unfavourable light in which our educated sons are regarded. Their interests are the same as our own, and it is only natural to expect that in all public matters they should be identified with us. It is also natural that having important matters to lay before His Excellency, after full consideration by ourselves, Councillors and people (both educated and uneducated), we should have the sar͠   ͠ ͠t in suitable shape by the writer thereof, and beg re   ͠lly that your Excellency might regard the sentiments ͠ rein as our own grievances and wants.

14. We desire also to bring to Your Excellency's notice the hardship on the inhabitants of Seccondee being shifted from site to site. The people of English Seccondee have been shifted once at much inconvenience, and they pray that their rumoured removal also from new English Seccondee (Essikadu) may be put a stop to. Equally would the people of Dutch Seccondee object to their being shifted from Accra Town which is at present occupied by them.

"We have the honour to be, Sir, your obedient servants,

ANAISI II., Omanhin Dutch Seccondee,
INKETSIA, Omanhin English Seccondee,
and others.

"Writer: CASELY HAYFORD,
Anona Chambers,
Seccondee.
" May 4, 1913."

—" The Gold Coast Nation," May 22 and 29, 1913.

APPENDIX C.

FURTHER DEPUTATION PRESS CORRESPONDENCE.

LANDS AND FORESTS IN WEST AFRICA.

To the Editor of " The Times."

Sir,—It would be obviously improper for us, under existing circumstances, to allow ourselves to be drawn into a controversy with the native gentlemen who have signed the letter in " The Times " of to-day. But lest confusion should arise in the public mind, the following facts may be usefully recorded.

Your correspondents are in this country to protest against a specific Ordinance brought forward by the Gold Coast Government after a detailed investigation by Mr. H. N. Thompson, Conservator of Forests, Southern Nigeria. [Cd.4993.] The principle with which this Ordinance is concerned is the preservation of certain forest areas in the Gold Coast and Ashanti from destruction and over-exploitation. We understand that the Secretary of State has received the deputation of protest, and has taken careful note of the arguments placed before him.

Partly as the result of a report [Cd.6278] on the system of alienation of native lands in the Gold Coast and Ashanti framed by Mr. Conway Belfield, who was appointed by Lord Crewe for the purpose, a Committee is now sitting to investigate the problem both as regards the Gold Coast and other parts of British West Africa.

Mr. Belfield was also instructed to furnish observations on the proposed Forest Ordinance. He did so. [Cd.6278.]

The Committee referred to has had your correspondents from West Africa before it, and has taken their evidence.

The question of the conservation of forest areas in the Gold Coast and the land question as a whole are, therefore, being carefully investigated and considered at this moment by a Committee, whose labours will, in the nature of the case, last many months.

Your obedient servants,

E. D. MOREL,
JOSIAH C. WEDGWOOD.
PHILIP MORRELL,
NOEL BUXTON,
ALBERT SPICER.

July 18.

GOLD COAST AFFAIRS.

Westminster Palace Hotel,

Victoria Street,

London, S.W.

To the Editor of the " African Mail."

Sir,—We notice the reproduction in your issue of 26th July, 1912, of the reply over the signatures of Messrs. E. D. Morel, Josiah C. Wedgwood, Philip Morrell, Noel Buxton, and Albert Spicer, to our letter in the " Times " of 18th July. Reluctant as we are to appear in print in any controversy bearing upon the Gold Coast Forest Bill, 1911, we are compelled to offer an explanation in view of the apparent Press campaign which you are vigorously waging against the interests of our people, whose real cause and true interests you seem to wholly misapprehend, much less to appreciate.

It being far from our intention to enter into any controversy in this matter with you and the other signatories to the letter under reference, who, by the way, are members of the West African Lands Committee, we did not reply to our said letter to " The Times."*

The position is too well understood to need any reminding that the enquiry into the Forest Bill, 1911, of the Gold Coast, and the West African Lands Committee's investigation into the system of land alienation in West Africa, with special reference to the Northern Nigeria land system, are not one and the same thing.

You and your co-signatories are not unaware that the Forest Ordinance of the Gold Coast, against which our people have protested, is drafted after the Forestry Ordinance of Nigeria.† And it must occur to you and them that the Forest Ordinance, the main principle of which is to compulsorily reserve the alleged " unoccupied " or " uncultivated " lands of the people and afterwards lease them to outsiders, cannot but have the effect of nationalising the lands of the people and of vesting ultimate ownerships thereof in the Crown, with whom, under the Bill, dealings with the lands must be negotiated. Such a system of land administration forms the basic principle of the one prevailing in Northern Nigeria, which is a conquered country, and which does not stand on the same footing as the Gold Coast, an unconquered, unceded, and unpurchased country.‡

Mr. Belfield, in his report on the Forest Bill, has, in the main, admitted the force of the people's contention, and recommended that the principle of compulsory reservation, and subsequent grant by way of lease to outsiders, should not be proceeded with by the Government. Upon this point Mr. Belfield says :—

" Certain portions of Sections 14, 15 and 16 appear to me to be open to grave objections, inasmuch as they indicate that when Government has secured the control of a forest area by the creation of a reserve, it proposes to lease or otherwise dispose of portions of it to third parties, or to give authority by way of licence to collect and remove forest produce. The declaration of such intention is one of the points which has aroused the hostility of the chiefs to the measure. They are not satisfied that Government will be content with using its powers merely to effect the collection of forest produce, but anticipate that once such powers have been taken, the reserves will be cut up and alienated as concessions or leased for purposes in no way connected with forest conservancy.

" Having regard to the wording of those sections, I should hesitate to say that such anticipations are devoid of foundation, and I think that the people have reason on their side in objecting to provisions which empower the Government to vest in other persons any interest in reserves of which it has undertaken the management."

Shortly after our arrival in this country* there appeared another article in " The Times " from the pen of its

Nigerian correspondent, who, we understand, is yourself. On the 19th July, the " African Mail," edited by you, in a leading article dealing with Mr. H. Conway Belfield's report, commented on it, and pointed out the desirability of introducing measures to check the alleged depletion of the forests, which we contend is not correct in view of the existing facts to the contrary, and also in view of an adverse criticism by Mr. G. D. Hazzledine on Mr. H. N. Thompson's report on the West African forests, which you caused to be published in your defunct journal, the " West African Mail," of October, 1904, now known as the " African Mail."† Mr. Belfield contradicts the alleged depletion of the forests in the following passage in his report :—

" The extent of land which has been alienated to Europeans in the Colony up to the present time bears no more than a very fractional proportion to the area which remains ; but in using the term ' alienated,' I must be understood to refer only to those properties the disposition of which has been formally completed by the issue of certificates of validity, and not to include the much more extensive area, in respect of which notices have been filed under the Concessions Ordinance, most of which have cumbered the books of the Court for many years, and of which only a small proportion will be further proceeded with."

Mr. Belfield publishes in his said report a valuable table from the Director of Surveys, giving details of the land disposed of year by year during the last decade. The approximate total area of the Colony is 24,300 square miles. Mr. Belfield further states in his said report :—" I believe it will be found that misconception, with regard to the area alienated, has arisen in the minds of people in England through inability to distinguish between those lands the disposition of which has been finally completed by the issue of certificates of validity, and those which are locally referred to as being ' under notice.' The latter are those in respect of which notice has been filed in accordance with the provisions of Section 9 of the Concessions Ordinance ; but in the vast majority of instances no further action is contemplated, and they continue to congest the Court records only because no efficient machinery has been provided for their removal. Still, so long as they are there, they must be included in any compilation of lands which are subject to the provisions of the Ordinance and within the cognisance of the Court, and as they aggregate in area a total exceeding 3,000 square miles, it is easy to understand that the inclusion of such figures in any return of lands alienated must convey a totally erroneous impression of the extent to which it has been disposed of.''‡

It is important to bear in mind that neither yourself nor any of the signatories to the letter under reference has been to the Gold Coast, and therefore you cannot be expected to know the conditions of the country as well as we do. It is not improbable that you and your co-signatories may have been misinformed as to the actual conditions there prevailing.§

You and your co-signatories may not know that the people of the soil have little or no representation on the Legislature of the country. Avenues of higher and other administrative appointments, which were open to the sons of the soil two or three generations ago, when the country had not reached its present state of development, are no longer open to them notwithstanding the spread of education and general knowledge and the vast economic development of the cocoa and other industries which has taken place in recent times.

It appears that much of the difficulty in this connection arises from a want of sympathy with the view of the sons of the soil as regards local conditions, and which can only be remedied by an adequate and independent representation on the Gold Coast Legislature.

These and the already unsatisfactory leave system of European officials, who invariably make short stay in the country through the frequent transfers to other Colonies just when they are beginning to understand the conditions of the place, whereby their successors are not infrequently compelled to follow up a subversive policy or abandon a useful one, must surely appear to you and your co-signatories that the people need to be more sympathised with and understood than the time-honoured way of treating the native view point of things that affect their material interests and welfare, as mere '' humbug.''

We deem it our duty to state that we did not give evidence before the West African Lands Committee as a deputation, as your letter would seem to suggest. In fact, when we were asked to do so we specially requested that our evidence might be taken not as members of the deputation, but as private individuals, our mission having no connection whatever with the said Committee.

From the last paragraph of your letter, it would appear that the Committee, of which you are members, has not only to deal incidentally with the Forest Ordinance, but also to deal with it specifically, and we are humbly of opinion that if justice is to be done to all parties, the other side of the question—that is, the people's case—must also be brought before the British public to enable it to form a correct view of the situation.

In conclusion, we regret to observe that whilst the matters under investigation are sub judice, you and your co-signatories, being members of the said Committee, should have written to the Press, pressing upon the public mind your views on the issues raised, on which you would have to report. ‖

We remain, Sir, your obedient servants,

T. F. E. JONES,
CASELY HAYFORD,
E. J. P. BROWN,
B. W. QUARTEY-PAPAFIO, M.D.

---

* The letter in the " Times " to which allusion is here made was itself by way of a brief reply to a long and controversial communication which the signatories in question declined to discuss in view of the appointment of the Land Committee.

† On the contrary, the draft legislation referred to differs in several important particulars from the Southern Nigerian Ordinance.

‡ No one has ever suggested that it did.

* The Deputation's arrival was, so far as we know, not publicly announced, and many persons interested in West African affairs were quite unaware of its presence in this country.

† Mr. Hazzledine is not an expert on tropical forestry. Mr. H. N. Thompson is one of the greatest living experts on the subject.

‖ This is precisely what the signatories of the letter in the " Times " declined to do, as set forth in the said letter. See footnote * (col. 1, p. 485).

APPENDIX D.

"THE REVIEW OF REVIEWS" AND THE FOREST BILL.

The following important reference to the Forest Bill occurred in the editorial columns of the *Review of Reviews* in its issue of August, 1912:—

" A question of native rights in the Gold Coast Colony has arisen out of the Forest Bill of 1911, and a deputation from the Native Chiefs and the million odd inhabitants is in London at the present time to voice the grievances of the natives in regard to it. Previous Bills met with the opposition of Kings and Chiefs, it being asserted that the rights of the natives would be interfered with. To a deputation to the Colonial Office in 1897, Mr. Chamberlain acknowledged the justice of the objections raised against the Bill, and it was prevented from becoming law. The present Bill also introduces similar encroachments, but under the name of management. If passed, it would give the Governor power to declare land subject to forest reservation ; to prohibit the taking of timber, rubber, etc., during certain periods ; and to constitute forest reserves. The deputation pleads that by taking away the control of the land from the Kings and Chiefs the whole fabric of native institutions will be destroyed. They cite the statement of the Conservator of Forests to show that the timber areas have scarcely been touched, that it is the native alone who is able to cultivate the soil to its utmost possibility, and that the European cannot dispense with him. It would, therefore, be a great mistake to deprive the native of the management of his own land. From time immemorial these lands have belonged to the natives, and it is by their labour that the great cocoa industry has been built up. If we wish them to remain independent and not suffer undue hardship, we ought to allow them the continued possession of their own land. It would be both unjust to those who are under our protection and contrary to the traditions of the British Empire were the British Government to be led away by the insidious whisperings of interested parties, and penalise the natives of the Gold Coast for their success in cocoa growing by destroying the whole fabric of their State constitution."

APPENDIX E.

The following able review appeared in " Transactions of the Royal Scottish Arboricultural Society," Vol. XXVI. part II., July, 1912 :—" Gold Coast Land Tenure and the Forest Bill, 1911. A review of the situation, by Casely Hayford, Barrister-at-Law." London : C. M. Phillips.

" The interesting pamphlet before us has been written with the view of enlisting the sympathy of the Colonial Office, Members of Parliament, and the people of this country in the case against this Bill, which has been ably stated by counsel, on behalf of the Kings and Chiefs and natives of the Gold Coast, at the Bar of the Legislative Council. The speeches of the various counsel engaged in the case, and the Governor's reply, are given in full. It appears that previous attempts at legislation on the same lines had been defeated owing to the opposition of the Kings and Chiefs, their main objection to the Bills being that each sought to infringe upon the inherent rights of the natives of the country in the ownership of their land. An attempt had apparently been made to show on behalf of the Government that there were waste and unoccupied—i.e., ownerless—lands in the country, but such a contention could not be upheld, and the various Bills never became law. The present Bill, it is asserted, introduces the same encroachments under the name of management. The Bill, if passed, would give the Governor in Council power to declare certain land subject to forest reservation ; to prohibit the taking of timber, rubber, etc., during certain periods ; to constitute forest reserves, and to manage native forest reserves. On behalf of the natives it was maintained that they could not understand the difference between management and confiscation. The Bill, they believe, would give the Government the whole power of management, and would sweep away the owners' rights to impose their own terms and conditions. It would seriously affect their inherent proprietary rights in the soil of their native land, and would tend to annihilate their social and political organisations and institutions. The Governor, in replying to the criticisms of the Bill, said that he thought the objections raised were based upon misapprehension of its terms, and he pointed out that the sole object of the Bill was to prevent the wasteful working and destruction of the forests of the Colony, the Government having not the slightest intention of taking away the lands of the people.

" The writer of the pamphlet goes on to draw conclusions from the facts that had been brought out in the discussion, insisting, first of all, that the land question of the Gold Coast and the principles appertaining to the tenure of the land had been finally settled by the Home Government long ago, and that it would be almost impossible to convince the natives that management such as is proposed under the Bill would not be a practical alienation of their rights in the land. It would be, he says, a disastrous error in policy to seek to alter in any material way the system of land tenure on the Gold Coast after the failure of various attempts which had been made in the past, because it is inconceivable to the native mind that any jurisdiction can exist without land and without the right and power of active management of such land. Take away the control of the land by the Kings and Chiefs, and you have practically destroyed the whole fabric of native institutions. If the Bill becomes law, lands might be reserved, and the real owner would have no right even to enter upon them without incurring a penalty, neither could he grant any concession without the Governor's consent, nor take any of the forest produce without a Government licence. As to the alleged destruction of the forests, he quotes the Conservator of Forests as saying that the timber areas had scarcely been touched. The same authority is also quoted to show that only the natives can successfully develop rubber planting. This, the writer says, puts the whole case in a nutshell. It is the native of the soil who must develop the possibilities of the soil, and, apart from him, European enterprise can do nothing; therefore to take over the management of the land from the native, and convert his condition into one little better than that which at one time prevailed in the Congo, would be a very bad blunder. The writer concludes with the following eloquent appeal: ' Please recognise the rights of indigenes ; please admit that they have a right to an opinion in a matter in which they are vitally interested. Let the principle of ' Live and let live ' be the guiding star in a constructive statesmanship, and all will be well. For, as His Excellency the Governor has wisely pointed out, even measure well pressed down, as between European capital and native labour, thus and only thus, will the land yield its increase for the betterment of all.'

" The whole controversy shows, on the one hand, that the natives are very jealous of their rights in their native land, and very suspicious of any action taken by the Government which might tend to alter or infringe upon those rights, which are so well defined and defended by the counsel engaged on their behalf ; and, on the other hand, it illustrates the difficulties which the Government have to deal with in trying to introduce amongst natives a system of forest management which these natives cannot understand, far less appreciate.   The opinion expressed by one of the counsel engaged in the case is worth recording.   What is required, he said in effect, are not forest officers to manage the forests, but well-trained instructors to instruct the Kings and Chiefs in the cultivation of their land.   Such forestry instructors might be appointed to educate the people in scientific agriculture and arboriculture.   These native Kings and Chiefs, having power under the native Jurisdiction Ordinance to make bye-laws for the conservation of the forests, could work hand in hand with such instructors, and be guided by their advice, to the lasting benefit of the economic development of the country."

INDEX.

INDEX.

ABEOKUTA, chiefs and people of, object to land policy of the Government, 84. Referred to 85.

Abokyi, captain, 137.

Aborigines Society—see Gold Coast Aborigines Rights Protection Society.

Abraham, Mr. J. D., 149, 172.

Abusa = a one-third share 57. When and in what respect payable, 57, 66.

Adams, Mr. W. H. quoted 27.

Adams, Mr., Acting Solicitor General, 75.

Addo, first King of Lagos, 17.

Addresses of Welcome, presented to the Governor at Cape Coast, by Aborigines Society on behalf of Kings and Chiefs of Central Province, 139 ; by Regent Tufuhin, Chiefs, etc., 142 ; by Town Council, 144. The Seccondee, 174.

" African Company of Merchants," referred to, 25. Committee of, despatch as to proceedings in Criminal trials, 27.

African Mail, quoted 8, 104, 181, referred to *passim*.

Africans in Africa, should they be kept apart ? 10.

African Times and Orient Review, referred to, 82, 92.

African (West) Exploitation and Development Syndicate, Limited v. Sir Alfred Kirby and others, cited, 54.

African World, referred to, 34. Quoted, 35.

Akataki people = the Commendas, 60. Originally came from *Akatakiwa*, 60. *Akataki* = masculine form, 60. *Akatakiwa* = feminine form, 60. Query, exact order of descent, 60. Branches of *Inkusukum* people, 60. Owe allegiance to Essandor, 60.

Alake of Yorubaland, 19, 20.

Allegiance, shown by payment of occasional contribution by subordinate chief to a paramount chief, 57. Fee, 57. An incident of paramountcy, 58, = *Personal* relationship between occupants of stools, 60. Acknowledged by military or other service, or fee, 60. Has nothing to do with lands, 60. Essential features of, 62. Penalty and result of transfer of, 62.

Aluko Onikoyi v. Jimba, Judgment in, referred to, 18.

Amba Danquah, Regent of Southern Assin, 61.